MW00887791

Court Officer
New York State
(Court Officer-Trainee)

FULL Practice Exams for 2020

Christopher W. Brandison

Note: NYS Court Officers start as "Court Officer-Trainees" and after two successful years are promoted to the rank of "Court Officer".

Unless otherwise stated, all passages in this book, including "rules" and "regulations", etc. and names of people and places are fictitious and have no connection with the NYS Unified Court System.

Copyright 2019 Christopher W. Brandison
All rights reserved.
ISBN: 9781673283952

"The will to win, the desire to succeed, the urge to reach your full potential...

these are the keys that will unlock the door to personal excellence."

- Confucius

Credits
 *   OCA sample written questions, 2014
(1) Wikipedia.org (edited)
(2) US Dept of State (Travel.state.gov)
(3) nycourts.gov

Contents

**All content prepared by former
NYS Court Officers and NYS Court Personnel**

GETTING READY FOR THE EXAM

The exam announcement for the 2020 exam states that the exam will be administered on the computer. If you don't have adequate experience using a computer, spend some time becoming familiar with the keyboard and reading information on the screen.

Also, if the computer assigned to you at the exam site doesn't work properly, immediately bring it to the attention of the test proctor.

The biggest misconception about the Court Officer-Trainee exam is that it is a "general knowledge exam" for which you don't really need to study.

The second biggest misconception is that the questions are easy.

Candidates who are convinced of the correctness of these two misconceptions usually go into the test unprepared and are quickly shocked - and depressed to see the unexpected high level of difficulty they must deal with.

Because of the difficulty of the exam, serious preparation is necessary if a candidate wishes to score high enough so that he does not have to wait for years to be canvassed for the pre-hiring screening process.

On the last exam, this means that to be canvassed within a reasonable time (and not at the last minute before the list expires, or not even canvassed) a score of 90 or above (within the NYC area) was required. Upstate, the score needed was in the 80s (due to fewer available candidates).

Our suggestion is that you study as early as possible - and as often as you can.

This book is a companion book to "NYS Court Officer-Trainee Exam Guide."
For maximum benefit (if you have time) study with both books.

You will notice that as you progress through the following pages and practice answering questions, you will greatly improve your performance.

"They can conquer who believe they can."

- Virgil, Roman poet

TYPES OF EXAM QUESTIONS

During the past 20 years, there usually have been five types of questions asked on the Court Officer-Trainee Exam:

- **Remembering Facts and Information**
- **Reading, Understanding and Interpreting Written Material**
- **Reading Comprehension and "Fill-ins" Questions**
- **Applying Facts and Information to Given Situations**
- **Clerical Checking**
- **Record Keeping**

All these questions lend themselves to being analyzed, so if you practice, you can improve your exam score.

Read the current exam announcement for any changes in the content or the administration of the exam.

In past years, the exams have been in written form. However, this year the test will be administered on the computer.

As you do each exam, try to improve your speed and accuracy.

Keep in mind that on the actual exam you may encounter some questions, such as the "table questions", that may have long columns of information and therefore will require more time to answer.

NOTE: This Court Officer-Trainee exam will be administered on the computer. Because of this, the instructions on how to answer the questions will vary.

- ☐ -

HINTS TO ACE THE EXAM

Remembering Facts and Information

Example of Directions

> **Directions: Read the brief story below. Study it for five minutes. You will then be instructed to wait for ten minutes before you answer the fifteen questions on the following page. Try to remember as many details of the incident without making any written notes."**

HINTS

1. Read the passage as many times as you can during the allotted five minutes.

2. Each time you read the passage, try to remember more and more details.

3. To help you remember better, try grouping the details into logical order. (For example, group the addresses, the names of people and places, and the time of day, etc. that are mentioned.)

   Examples:

   Addresses: (30 Wilken St., 46 Elmont Ave., 59 Grand Pkwy., etc.)

   Names of people: (Baker, Devon, Jamieson, Martinoff, etc.)

   Time of day: (9:00 a.m., 11:50 a.m., 2:45 p.m., 5:00 p.m., etc.)

4. If you find it helpful, briefly close your eyes after each reading and try to remember or visualize what you have read.

5. After you are no longer allowed to look at the passage, try to keep the details fresh in your mind. During the approximately 10 minutes pause before you will be allowed to answer the questions, do not get overly distracted by what might be happening around you.

6. After you answer the memory test questions, do not change your answer unless you are confident and reasonably certain that you are replacing a wrong answer with a correct answer and not replacing it with just a guess or gut-feeling. In other words, stick with your first answer unless you have a good reason to change it.

You can practice the above techniques every day by selecting a passage (about 400 words) from a newspaper or book and reading it for five minutes. After five minutes, wait another ten minutes and then write down as many details as you can remember. By practicing daily, your memory and your approach to this type of question will probably greatly improve.

Reading, Understanding and Interpreting Written Material

FORMAT A: Reading Comprehension

Example of Directions

> **"Directions: After reading the selection below, choose the alternative which best answers the question following the selection."***

HINTS

In this format, each question contains a brief reading selection followed by a question or questions pertaining to the information in the selection. All the information required to answer the question(s) is provided, so even if the reading selection is on a topic with which you are not familiar, you will be able to answer the question(s) by reading the selection carefully. Remember, answer the questions based only on the information you read in the selection. Do not use any prior knowledge that you may have on the subject in choosing your answers."*

Questions relating to the content of short passages are usually easier to answer than questions relating to much longer passages. The key here is to take the time to carefully read the passage. Some candidates like to first skim the passage to get an overall general understanding of what is being said. After that (or sometimes even before skimming the passage) some candidates like to glance at the question(s) to see what sections of the passage are more important than others. Whichever method you wish to use, you must strive to understand what is being conveyed.

A quick, fuzzy reading of the passage is usually not enough to answer all the questions correctly. Therefore, read the passage again, more carefully this time, and continue to read it as many times as you need within the time limits of the exam. When you select an answer choice, confirm that you are selecting it because there is something in the passage that makes this choice correct and all the other choices incorrect. A "general feeling" that you are selecting the correct choice is not enough.

FORMAT B: "Fill-in" Questions

Example of Directions

"Directions: The three passages below each contain five numbered blanks. Below each passage are listed five sets of words numbered to match the blanks. Pick the word from each set which seems to make the most sense both in the sentence and the total paragraph."*

HINTS

"In this format the test contains a short, written passage from which some words have been omitted. You need to select one word from the four alternatives that best completes the passage."*

In selecting the correct word to place in the blank, keep in mind that a choice may be correct (or incorrect) because of one or more of the following reasons:

1. SPELLING: Is the word spelled correctly?

   preceed? precede? preeseed? prisede? ("precede" is spelled correctly)

2. VOCABULARY: Is the meaning of the word appropriate?

   capital (city), capitol (building)

   "to" (direction), "too" (excessive), "two" (number)

3. GRAMMAR: run-on sentence, sentence fragment, singular or plural? past or present tense?

   Run-on sentence: "The boy walked the girl ran."

   Correct version: "The boy walked. The girl ran."

   Another correct way to say it, "The boy walked and the girl ran."

   Singular or plural: Not correct: The boy walk very fast. ("walk" should be "walks" because boy is singular (one) and walks is a singular verb. Correct: "The boy walks fast."

4. LOGIC OF SENTENCE (agreement with the logic of whatever is being said in the passage.)

   Not correct: "The boy accumulated many marbles because he was good at the game. By evening he had (more? / less?) marbles than when he started in the morning.

   The correct choice is "more" because during the day he accumulated ("acquired an increasing number") of marbles.

Applying Facts and Information to Given Situations

Example of Directions

"Directions: Use the information preceding each question to answer the question. Only that information should be used in answering the questions. Do not use any prior knowledge you may have on the subject. Choose the alternative that best answers the question."*

HINTS

"This section of the written exam assesses your ability to take information which you have read and apply it to a specific situation defined by a given set of facts. Each question contains a brief paragraph which describes a regulation, procedure or law. The selection is followed by a description of a specific situation. Then a question is asked which requires you to apply the law, regulation, or procedure described in the paragraph to the specific situation. Remember that all of the information you need to answer the question is contained in the paragraph and in the description of the situation. You need to read and understand both before you attempt to answer the question."*

1. When answering this type of question, a candidate must be careful not to choose an answer based on the candidate's experiences. Select the answer based only on the rule or procedure and the situation that is stated.

2. If the rule or procedure lists steps that must be taken in a specific order, make sure that you choose an answer that does not violate that order.

3. If the rules or procedures are complicated, you may want to jot down details that you feel will help you answer the questions.

Clerical Checking

Example of Directions

Directions: The following example consists of three sets of information. Compare the information in the three sets. On your answer sheet, mark:

Choice A: if none of the three sets are exactly alike

Choice B: if only the first and second sets are exactly alike

Choice C: if only the first and third sets are exactly alike

Choice D: if all the sets are exactly alike.

HINTS

"This section of the examination assesses your ability to determine whether different sets of words, numbers, names and codes are similar. No matter what the form of the item, you are required to scan the sets of information, identify where the sets differ, and use the directions to determine the correct answer."*

This type of question might at first glance seem easy. However, it is relatively tricky, especially if you are not a careful reader. This is the type of question where the correct answer is right in front of you. All you have to do is recognize it.

1. Read the description of the answer choices carefully. It is very easy to mix-up the descriptions if you read too quickly or are nervous during the test.

2. If possible, try to keep your finger on the information line (or use a pencil, or sheet of paper under the line to help guide your eyes).

3. Do not read the lines as you would read a novel. Compare a section of the information that is not too long or too short.

   For example, compare "1973 Elks" in the first column to "1973 Elks" in the second and third columns, instead of trying to compare "1973 Elks Dr. S.W." all at once.

4. Different fonts (styles of print) may make the information "look different," but they do NOT change the information.

   For example, the information in "*1284 Elcome Street*" is THE SAME INFORMATION as in

   "*1284 Elcome Street*"

Record Keeping

Example of Directions

> "Directions: Answer the five questions based on the information contained in the following tables. Remember, all of the information needed to answer the questions correctly can be found in the tables. Complete the "Daily Breakdown of Cases" and "Summary of Cases" tables before you attempt to answer any of the questions."*

HINTS

"These questions will assess your ability to read, combine and manipulate written information organized from several different sources."*

The key to maximizing your score on this type of "Table" question is to practice as much as possible. By doing this, you will develop an "approach" to answering the questions and develop the necessary speed and accuracy that you will need on the actual test.

Please note that some questions may be answered without having to fill-in the blank supplemental tables that are provided. However, for other questions, you will definitely need to have the supplemental tables filled in, especially when the information tables are long (20-25 rows). Our suggestion is not to try to manage with "short-cuts." Fill-in the supplemental table.

A variation of the above Record Keeping questions involves them supplying you with a table where some information boxes need to be filled-in. The key to this type of question is to understand the structure of the table and the relationships of the information among the rows and columns. You may be asked to determine the values of the missing numbers and then answer questions based on the completed table.

Example: Fill in the missing blanks (1-5).

Number of Cases Handled In Parts A-D

Part	Monday	Tuesday	Wednesday	Thursday	Friday	Total
A	5	(1)	7	9	6	(2)
B	6	9	9	5	8	37
C	9	5	8	6	(5)	37
D	7	6	(4)	7	5	34
Total	(3)	28	33	27	28	143

Answers (1-5)

1. 8   2. 35   3. 27   4. 9   5. 9

PRACTICE TEST 1: QUESTIONS
(75 Questions: Time allowed: 3.5 hours)

Questions 1-15: Remembering Facts and Information

"Directions: Read the brief story below. Study it for five minutes. Then, turn the story over and wait for ten minutes before you answer the fifteen questions on the following page. Try to remember as many details of the incident without making any written notes."*

(**Written test:** At the end of the five minutes, the test monitor will collect this sheet and ten minutes after that, you will be instructed to begin the test by answering from memory the first fifteen questions relating to this story.

Computer test: At the end of the five minutes, the passage will disappear from the screen and ten minutes after that, you will be instructed to begin the test by answering from memory the first fifteen questions relating to this story.)

On Thursday, November 14, 2019, five Court Officer-Trainees reported to their first assignment, the Family Court in Westbury (in Nassau County) New York. All five officers were pleased with their assignment because they all lived in Nassau and the daily commute to work for all of them would be brief. Three of the officers were women and two were men. All were less than forty years old.

One of them, Janet Franklin, was a six year veteran of the New York City Police Department. Although she liked her police job, she found that the irregular shifts and assignments created a hardship on her two young children who attended elementary school. Because of this, she decided to take the Court Officer-Trainee exam and was pleased when she learned that she had passed the test with a score of ninety-seven.

The youngest of the five officers, Nicole Hastings, was twenty-one years old. The Court Officer-Trainee job was her first full-time position. She had taken the test when she was eighteen. Her father was a retired Court Officer and always encouraged her to work in civil service, particularly as a peace officer.

The other female officer, Diane Cavuto, had taken the exam when she was working as a Clerical Office Assistant in the same court where she was now assigned as a Court Officer-Trainee. Officer Cavuto was thrilled at the opportunity to serve her community as an officer of the court.

The other two Court Officer-Trainees were males in their thirties. One of them had worked in banks and the other had extensive experience in sales. Although each had enjoyed his job, they decided that the Court Officer job offered more opportunity to serve the public while at the same time earning valuable benefits, including a very desirable pension.

All the officers reported at 9:00 a.m. to the Major's Office on the seventh floor of the Family Court building. Major Thomas Patterson greeted them with a friendly smile and wished them well as they started their two-year Court Officer continuing training.

Answer questions 1-15 based on the information provided in the passage which you have read.

1. At what time did the five officers report to the Major's Office?

A. 9:00 p.m.

B. 8:00 a.m.

C. 9:10 a.m.

D. 9:00 a.m.

2. What is the last name of the youngest officer?

A. Cavern

B. Hamilton

C. Hastings

D. Peterson

3. How old is the youngest officer?

A. 20

B. 21

C. 18

D. 22

4. On what date did the officers report to their assigned court?

A. 10/4/2019

B. 10/14/2019

C. 11/4/19

D. 11/14/2019

5. The assigned court is located in which of the following?

A. West Burlington

B. West Hampton

C. Westbury

D. Westburn

6. How many of the officers were women?

A. 2

B. 3

C. 1

D. 4

7. Which officer scored 97 on the Court Officer-Trainee test?

A. Hamilton

B. Franklin

C. Jamison

D. Harling

8. Which officer had taken the exam when she was working as a Clerical Office Assistant?

A. Franklin

B. Corning

C. Madison

D. Cavuto

9. The two male officers were in their _____.

A. twenties   C. forties

B. thirties   D. none of the above

10. The Major's Office is located on the _____ floor.

A. fourth   C. second

B. sixth   D. seventh

11. One of the officers was a _____ year veteran of the New York City Police Department.

A. four   C. six

B. five   D. seven

12. The last name of the Major is _____.

A. Peterson   C. Parkinson

B. Patterson   D. none of the above

13. The last name of the officer whose father was a retired Court Officer is _____.

A. Hamilton   C. Hastings

B. Carsons   D. Peterson

14. The last name of the officer with two school-age children is _____.

A. Benjamin   C. Hamilton

B. Madison   D. Franklin

15. All five officers lived in _____.

A. Eastbury   C. Nassau

B. Eastbery   D. Mulberry

▲

Questions 16 - 30: Reading, Understanding and Interpreting Written Material

"Directions: The three passages below each contain five numbered blanks. Below each passage are listed five sets of words numbered to match the blanks. Pick the word from each set which seems to make the most sense both in the sentence and the total paragraph."*

Passage 1

Since it is not possible to know with ___16___ the extent to which something is 'secure' (and a measure of vulnerability is unavoidable), perceptions of security vary, often greatly. For example, a fear of death by earthquake is common in the United States (US), but ___17___ on the bathroom floor kills more people; and in France, the United Kingdom and the US there are far fewer deaths caused by ___18___ than there are women killed by their partners in the home.

Another ___19___ of perception is the common assumption that the mere presence of a security system (such as armed forces, or antivirus software) implies security. For example, ___20___ computer security programs installed on the same device can prevent each other from working properly, while the user assumes that he or she benefits from twice the protection that only one program would afford.(1)

16.	17.	18.	19.	20.
a. prisision	a. dripping	a. terorism	a. examples	a. one
b. presecion	b. billking	b. terrerism	b. problem	b. a
c. prisicion	c. slipping	c. tearerism	c. variables	c. two
d. precision	d. slapping	d. terrorism	d. problems	d. sole

Passage 2

Security lighting is another effective form of deterrence. Intruders are less likely to ___21___ well-lit areas for fear of being seen. Doors, gates, and other entrances, in particular, should be ___22___ to allow close observation of people entering and exiting. When lighting the grounds of a ___23___, widely distributed low-intensity lighting is generally superior to small patches of high-intensity lighting, because the latter can have a tendency to create blind spots for security personnel and CCTV cameras. It is important to place lighting in a manner that makes it difficult to tamper with (e.g. suspending lights from ___24___ poles), and to ___25___ that there is a backup power supply so that security lights will not go out if the electricity is cut off. (1)

21.	22.	23.	24.	25.
a. exit	a. unlit	a. facelity	a. short	a. insure
b. avoid	b. dim	b. facility	b. tall	b. ensur
c. enter	c. lightless	c. fasility	c. little	c. insur
d. hinder	d. well lit	d. facillity	d. petite	d. ensure

Passage 3

Research has ___26___ evidence that second-hand smoke causes the same problems as direct smoking, including lung cancer, cardiovascular disease, and lung ailments such as emphysema, ___27___, and asthma. Specifically, meta-analyses show that lifelong non-smokers with partners who smoke in the home ___28___ a 20–30% greater risk of lung cancer than non-smokers who live with non-smokers. Non-smokers ___29___ to cigarette smoke in the workplace have an increased lung cancer risk of 16–19%. Several well-established carcinogens have been shown by the tobacco companies' own ___30___ to be present at higher concentrations in second-hand smoke than in mainstream smoke.(1)

26.	27.	28.	29.	30.
a. decreased	a. bronkitis	a. accepts	a. imposed	a. opinion
b. lessened	b. bronkiatis	b. has	b. exposed	b. flak
c. reduced	c. bronchitis	c. acquires	c. shunned	c. research
d. generated	d. brokitis	d. have	d. expose	d. estimate

Questions 31 - 35: Applying Facts and Information to Given Situations

"Directions: Use the information preceding each question to answer the question. Only that information should be used in answering the questions. Do not use any prior knowledge you may have on the subject. Choose the alternative that best answers the question."*

Answer Questions 31 and 32 based on the following procedure and situations.

"DHS Suspicious Item Procedure

1. Do NOT touch, tamper with, or move the package, bag, or item.
2. Notify authorities immediately: Notify your facility supervisor, such as a manager, operator, or administrator, or follow your facility's standard operating procedure.
3. Call 9-1-1 or your local law enforcement if no facility supervisor is available.
4. Explain why it appears suspicious.
5. Follow instructions. Facility supervisors and/or law enforcement will assess the situation and provide

guidance regarding shelter-in-place or evacuation.

6. If no guidance is provided and you feel you are in immediate danger, calmly evacuate the area. Distance and protective cover are the best ways to reduce injury from a bomb.

7. Be aware. There could be other threats or suspicious items."(2)

Question 31
Situation

On Monday morning, while Court Officer-Trainee Peter Bronfaro is on his way from the Court Officer Operations Office to his assigned part on the second floor, he notices a suspicious cardboard package in the stairwell near the second floor landing. Although no noise is coming out of it, a strange chemical smell is in the air. Officer Bronfaro concludes that the package is suspicious and that he needs to proceed according to the DHS Suspicious Item Procedure.

31. Based on the preceding procedure and situation, which of the following choices is the best course of action that Officer Bronfaro should take?

A. Quickly ask the persons in the second floor hallway if the package belongs to any of them.

B. Pick up the package to estimate its weight and also smell it to see if the smell is the same as the smell that is in the air.

C. Immediately call 911, as there is no time to lose.

D. None of the above

Question 32
Situation

On a different day, after Court Officer-Trainee Nancy Williams unlocks the front door of her empty courtroom, room 404 on the fourth floor, she notices a shoe-sized box in the back of the room. A loud ticking noise is coming out of it. Outside, in the hallway, there are more than twenty people waiting to enter the courtroom. Officer Williams immediately notifies the Major in the Court Officer Operations Office on the third floor who advises her to keep the public away from the box.

32. Based on the preceding procedure and situation, which of the following is the next best course of action that Officer Williams should take?

A. Immediately take the box into the back room of the courtroom, as this would decrease injuries to the public if there were a bomb in the box and it exploded.

B. Make an announcement to immediately evacuate the second floor.

C. Make an announcement to immediately evacuate the second floor (and the first and third floors).

D. Follow the Major's orders, wait for her Court Officer Supervisor and follow the supervisor's further directions.

Answer Questions 33 - 35 are based on the following procedure and situations.

Procedure when a court officer is required to wear a Body-Worn Camera (BWC)

1. When putting on the uniform prior to a shift:

   a. Retrieve from the Operations Office your assigned BWC from its charging station.

   b. Inspect the BWC to make sure that it is fully charged.

2. Attach the BWC to the outermost garment, in the center of the chest using the clip-on mount provided.

3. Document the successful completion of steps 1 and 2 in the Master BWC Log. Note any problems with the BWC.

4. Activate BWC at the start of your tour.

5. Before responding to a scene, check that the BWC is functioning (Blue light should be on.)

6. At the scene, unless it would be impracticable or unsafe to do so, notify the public that your BWC is recording.

7. Do not turn off the BWC unless directed to do so by a supervising officer.

8. Any problems with the operation of the BWC must be brought to the attention of the Operations Office as soon as possible.

Situation 1

Court Officer-Trainee Derek Cummings, the rookie at his court, reported to the Operations Office at 9:00 a.m. to obtain a BWC unit for the day. He is issued Unit 27. When he attempts to put it on, he notices that the clip-on mount is missing and has been replaced with a paper clip.

33. Based on the preceding BWC procedure and preceding situation, which of the following is the best course of action that Officer Cummings should follow?

A. Use the paperclip and don't mention it because it obviously is the way that this unit has been worn and he is the rookie and he should not complain.

B. Complain to his supervisor that he is being issued defective equipment because he is the rookie.

C. Ask for another paperclip so that he can secure the BWC better on his shirt.

D. He should inform his supervisor and note the missing clip-on mount in the Master BWC book.

Situation 2

Later in the day, Court Officer-Trainee Georgina Hamilton, responds to a complaint that in the third floor hallway, a male in his fifties is threatening to take all his clothes off because "his ex-wife has taken everything else from him." When she arrives at the scene, the man is in the process of taking his clothes off.

34. Based on the BWC procedure and the preceding situation, what is the best course of action for Officer Hamilton to take?

A. Turn the camera to such an angle that it will not record the naked man.

B. Notify the man and the public that her BWC is recording.

C. Officer Hamilton should leave the scene so as to not record nudity.

D. Contact headquarters and ask them to send an officer without a BWC.

Situation 3

Court Officer-Trainee Roberto Gomez is on roaming security at 4:15 p.m. when he notices that the blue light on his BWC has turned red.

35. Based on the BWC procedure and the preceding situation, what is the best first course of action for Officer Gomez to take?

A. Take off his BWC so as to not draw "looks" from the public.

B. Turn off the BWC.

C. Dismantle and try to repair the BWC.

D. Bring the malfunction to the attention of the Operations Office as soon as possible.

▲

For questions 36 - 40, read the following passage and then answer the questions based solely on the information provided in the passage.

New York police officers may arrest someone they have reason to believe has committed a felony, misdemeanor, or violation, or pursuant to an arrest warrant. Those arrested are booked at "central booking" and interviewed by a representative of the Criminal Justice Agency for the purposes of recommending bail or remand at arraignment. In New York state, the time from arrest to arraignment must be within 24 hours. Police may also release a person with an appearance ticket directing a defendant to appear for arraignment in the future: with a desk appearance ticket (DAT) after arrest, or a universal summons without arrest.

At arraignment, the accused is informed of the charges against them and submits a plea (and may accept a plea bargain). The accused have a right to be represented by a lawyer, and one will be appointed for them if they cannot afford one. Arraignments are held every day from 9:00 am to 1:00 am. At arraignment the prosecutor may also provide defense counsel with certain "notices", such as notices about police lineups and statements made by the defendant to police.

After notices are served, the prosecutor may ask the court to keep the accused in jail (remanded) or released on bail. Otherwise, the accused is released on their own recognizance (ROR'd). If the accused is released, the accused must appear in court every time their case is calendared (scheduled for a court hearing), and if they fail to appear, the judge may forfeit their bail and issue a bench warrant for their arrest, although judges may excuse defendants from having to show up at every court appearance.

The decision to set bail and the amount of bail to set are discretionary, and the central issue regarding bail is insuring the defendant's future appearances in court; factors to be taken into consideration are defined in Criminal Procedure Law Section 510.30. In practice, bail amounts are typically linked to charge severity rather than risk of failure to appear in court. Judges overwhelmingly rely only on cash bail and commercial bail bonds instead of other forms of bail, and courts rarely inquire into the defendant's financial resources to understand what amount of bail might be securable by them.(1)

36. Which of the following statements is not supported by the above passage?

A. Bail factors are defined in Civil Procedure Law Section 510.30.

B. New York police officers may arrest someone they have reason to believe committed a violation.

C. Bail amounts are typically linked to charge severity.

D. Cash bail and commercial bail bonds are overwhelmingly relied upon by Judges.

37. Which of the following statements is supported by the above passage? At arraignment:

A. the defendant cannot accept a plea bargain.

B. the defendant must be represented by a lawyer appointed for them.

C. the amount of bail is discretionary with the Judge.

D. None of the above statements are supported by the passage.

38. Which of the following is correct? The amount of bail is set by:

A. the Criminal Justice Agency

B. the DA

C. the Judge

D. the arresting police officer

39. A "calendared" case is a case that:

A. is more than one year old.

B. is on every month of the year.

C. is on where bail has been set.

D. is scheduled for a court hearing.

40. Which of the following statements is correct? Arraignments:

A. are held from 9:00 am to 1:00 pm

B. are where the accused are convicted of the charges against them.

C. are where the accused always proceed without a lawyer

D. are held every day

Questions 41 - 60: Clerical Checking

Directions: The following example consists of five sets of information.

Compare the information in the three sets, and on your answer sheet, mark:

Choice A: if none of the three sets are exactly alike

Choice B: if only the second and third sets are exactly alike

Choice C: if only the first and second sets are exactly alike

Choice D: if all the sets are exactly alike

41. Weinford Ave. W. Supreme Court, NYC Justice J. Harrison ID: 73974-295389	41. Weinford Ave. W. Supreme Court, NYC Justice J. Harrison **ID: 73974-295398**	41. *Weinferd Ave. W.* Supreme Court, NYC Justice J. Harrison ID: 73974-295389
42. Gorges, Jakes, et al. CPLR 1021.2 (a-b) 8439-287 Eiker St. *Westchester, Beacon*	42. Gorges, Jakes, et al. CPLR 1021.2 (a-b) 8439-287 Eiker St. *Westchester, Beacon*	42. Gorges, Jakes, et al. CPLR 1021.2 (a-b) 8439-287 Eiker St. *Westchester, Beacon*
43. 353813-798534128 **Rooms 17C and 22A** 3/12/18 and 5/14/19 73 Belton Avenue	43. 353813-798534128 Rooms 17C and 22A 3/12/18 and 5/14/19 73 Belton Avenue	43. 353813-798534128 Rooms 17D and 22A 3/12/18 and 5/14/19 73 Belton Avenue
44. Sergeant L. Ulmer PL: 1002, 7528 (b) Witness Jane Venton C: 28394-36886356	44. Sergeant L. Ulmer PL: 1002, 7528 (b) *Witness Jane Venton* C: 28394-36886356	44. Sergeant L. Ulmer PL: 1002, 7528 (b) Witness Jane Venton C: 28394-36886536
45. Military Calendar Clerk Mary Rodrigues Hearing Examiners Samuel G. Olsted	45. Military Calendar Clerk Mary Rodriguez Hearing Examiners Samuel G. Olsted	45. Military Calendar Clerk Mary Rodriguez **Hearing Examiners** Samuel G. Olsted

Directions: The following example consists of five sets of information. Compare the information in the three sets, and on your answer sheet, mark:

Choice A: if all the sets are exactly alike.

Choice B: if only the second and third sets are exactly alike

Choice C: if only the first and second sets are exactly alike

Choice D: if none of the three sets are exactly alike

46. 243 Central Avenue **Court Attorney Jones** Rms. 205, 301, 407 MHL 9002.43 (d - e)	46. 243 Central Avenue Court Attorney Jones Rms. 205, 301, 407 MHL 9002.43 (d - e)	46. 243 Central Avenue Court Attorney Jones Rms. 205, 301, 407 MHL 9002.43 (d - e)
47. TBA 12/15/2019 JHO Harriet Chang Report: SR2825EH Priority 7A, 8B, 9G	47. TBA 12/15/2019 JHO Harriet Chang **Report: SR2855EH** Priority 7A, 8B, 9G	47. TBA 12/15/2019 JHO Harriet Chang Report: SR2855EH Priority 7A, 88, 9G
48. CPL Sect. 75.3 (g) Attorney B. Sheldon Control 287452-19 Report Ref. 42G (h)	48. CPL Sect. 75.3 (g) Attorney B. Sheldon Control 287452-19 Report Ref. 42G (h)	48. CPL Sect. 75.3 (g) Attorney B. Sheldon Control 287452-19 Report Ref. 42G (n)
49. Probate Room 201 Vorliotis, Francis Locations: 3017 (a-h) *Richmond, NY 10365*	49. Probate Room 201 Vorliotis, Frances Locations: 3017 (a-h) Richmond, NY 10365	49. Probate Room 201 Vorliotis, Frances Locations: 3017 (a-h) Richmond, NY 10365
50. 3877 Dakota Street *Marianoti, Ellena* Queens and Bronx Sonya T. Arianof	50. 3877 Dakota Street *Marianoti, Ellena* Queens and Bronx Sonya T. Arianoff	50. 3877 Dakota Street *Marianoti, Ellena* Queens and Bronx **Sonya T. Arianoff**

Directions: The following example consists of five sets of information. Compare the information in the three sets, and on your answer sheet, mark:

Choice A: if only the first and second sets are exactly alike

Choice B: if only the second and third sets are exactly alike

Choice C: if all the sets are exactly alike.

Choice D: if none of the three sets are exactly alike

51. IG Rep. SF 214-284 29 Court Officers **Magistrate C. Loman** Connie S. Malvinotta	51. IG Rep. SF 214-284 29 Court Officers Magistrate C. Loman Connie S. Malvinotta	51. IG Rep. SF 214-284 29 Court Officers Magistrate C. Loman Connie S. Malvinotta
52. Locations (284-342) Police Precinct 101 Court Reporter Inger Sergeant W. Strand	52. Locations (284-342) *Police Precinct 101* Court Reporter Inger Sergeant W. Strand	52. Locations (284-342) Police Precint 101 Court Reporter Inger Sergeant W. Strand
53. 2795 Furman Street EPTL 1826 & 7938 Ingerman, William Diary 5/18/19 - 7/5/19	53. 2795 Furman Street EPTL 1826 & 7938 **Ingerman, William** Diary 5/13/19 - 7/5/19	53. 2795 Furman Street EPTL 1826 & 7938 Ingerman, William Diary 5/13/19 - 7/5/19
54. Hazelton, Gold, Brat SS Code 3948-39571 *SPCA Codes A-F* Mediator A. Mingano	54. Hazelton, Gold, Brat SS Code 3948-39571 SPCA Codes A-F Mediator A. Mimgano	54. Hazelton, Gold, Brat SS Code 3948-39571 SPCA Codes A-F Mediator A. Mingamo
55. Lincoln Circle West 254-397 Elder Street NYSC Report 2019 2422581/2019 (v)	55. Lincoln Circle West 254-397 Elder Street NYSC Report 2019 2422581/2019 (v)	55. Lincoln Circle West 254-397 Eldert Street **NYSC Report 2019** 2422581/2019 (v)

Directions: The following example consists of five sets of information. Compare the information in the three sets, and on your answer sheet, mark:

Choice A: if only the second and third sets are exactly alike

Choice B: if only the first and second sets are exactly alike

Choice C: if all the sets are exactly alike.

Choice D: if none of the three sets are exactly alike

56. *Court Rep. Davidson* 236-369 Weiner St. Elkor Management Smith St., Brooklyn	56. *Court Rep. Davidson* 236-369 Weiner St. Elkor Management Smith St., Brooklyn	56. *Court Rep. Davison* 236-369 Weiner St. Elkor *Management* Smith St., Brooklyn
57. 357-51 Miriam Street Probated Section 13 **Tax Ref. 2019-27492** Supervisor B. Donner	57. 357-51 Miriam Street Probated Section 13 Tax Ref. 2019-27492 Supervisor B. Donner	57. 357-51 Miriam Street Probate Section 13 Tax Ref. 2019-27492 Supervisor B. Donner
58. 38666/19, 48875/19 5931 Lincoln Ave. PINS Part 205 (H) 635813147-62389	58. 38666/19, 48875/19 5931 Lincoln Ave. PINS Part 205 (H) 6358131147-62389	58. 38666/19, 48875/19 5931 Lincoln Ave. PINS Part 205 (H) 6358131147-62389
59. Tom Lomer (Albany) Tracking3675544248 *Plaintiff Gail James* Accounting, Rm. 243	59. Tom Lomer (Albany) Tracking3675544248 Plaintiff Gail James Accounting, Rm. 243	59. Tom Lomer (Albany) Tracking3675544248 **Plaintiff Gail James** Accounting, Rm. 243
60. Family Center 205 (b) File CRIM 3245/2019 Judge Tania Jimenez Albany and Niagara	60. Family Center 205 (b) File CRIM 3245/2019 Judge Tania Jimenez Albany and Niagara	60. Family Center 205 (d) File CRIM 3245/2019 Judge Tania Jimenez Albany and Niagara

Questions 61-75: Record Keeping

The following pages contain the following:

1. Three individual tables listing cases that appeared before Trial Judges

in Criminal, Family, Civil Courts (November 4, 2019 - November 8, 2019).

2. A coding table "Coding Table: Part / Judge Presiding".

3. Two summary tables to organize the information presented in the

first three tables listing cases that appeared before Judges in

Criminal, Family, Civil Courts (November 4, 2019 - November 8, 2019).

Directions: Complete the two summary tables based on the information provided and then answer the ten questions that follow. Note that only the answers to the ten questions will be graded and not the work done on the tables.

Criminal Court List of Cases On the Court Calendar November 4, 2019 - November 8, 2019			
Judge Presiding	**Date Case Filed**	**Case Disposition**	**Fine Imposed**
Baranov	12/6/17	Dismissed	
Einfeld	5/24/18	Trial	$ 1,500
Baranov	12/3/17	Adjourned	
Einfeld	8/11/18	Dismissed	
Baranov	2/4/19	Trial	--
Einfeld	4/12/18	Defaulted	
Einfeld	4/22/18	Adjourned	
Baranov	1/7/19	Trial	--
Baranov	3/25/19	Dismissed	
Einfeld	3/27/19	Adjourned	
Baranov	6/17/19	Trial	$ 2,500
Einfeld	8/24/19	Adjourned	

Coding Table	
Part / Judge Presiding	
Part	**Judge Presiding**
C2	Brendais
C8	Abram
F3	Chin
F4	Romano
R5	Einfeld
R7	Baranov

Family Court			
List of Cases On the Court Calendar			
November 4, 2019 - November 8, 2019			
Judge Presiding	**Date Case Filed**	**Case Disposition**	**Amount of Restitution Ordered**
Romano	12/4/18	Adjourned	
Chin	12/9/18	Trial	$ 750
Romano	12/22/18	Dismissed	
Romano	1/25/19	Trial	$ 1,500
Chin	1/29/19	Dismissed	
Romano	2/5/19	Adjourned	
Chin	6/22/19	Trial	---
Chin	7/14/19	Trial	$ 1,250
Romano	8/25/19	Dismissed	
Chin	8/29/19	Trial	$ 1,000
Romano	9/2/19	Dismissed	
Chin	9/6/19	Adjourned	

Civil Court			
List of Cases On the Court Calendar			
November 4, 2019 - November 8, 2019			
Judge Presiding	Date Case Filed	Case Disposition	Settlement Award Amount
Brendais	3/24/17	Settled	$ 3,500
Abram	4/19/17	Adjourned	
Abram	3/16/18	Adjourned	
Brendais	4/21/18	Dismissed	
Abram	7/3/18	Settled	$ 12,500
Brendais	2/21/19	Adjourned	
Abram	3/17/19	Settled	
Brendais	4/13/19	Adjourned	
Abram	6/12/19	Settled	$ 9,500
Brendais	6/15/19	Adjourned	
Brendais	6/18/19	Settled	

(Summary Tables 1 and 2 are on the following two pages.)

――――――――――

Summary Table 1:

Cases on Calendar November 4, 2019 - November 8, 2019				
Case Status	**Criminal**	**Family**	**Civil**	**Total Cases**
Adjourned				
Defaulted				
Dismissed				
Settled - with Money Award				
Settled - no money award				
Trial with Fine Imposed				
Trial with no fine imposed				
Trial with Restitution Ordered				
Trial with no Restitution Ordered				
Total Cases				
Cases by Date Filed				
2017				
2018				
2019				
Total Cases				

Summary Table 2:

<table>
<tr><th colspan="7">Cases on Calendar
November 4, 2019 - November 8, 2019</th></tr>
<tr><td></td><th colspan="6">Case Status at End of Day</th></tr>
<tr><th>Part Code</th><th>Adjourned</th><th>Defaulted</th><th>Dismissed</th><th>Settled Money Award</th><th>Trial with Fine Imposed</th><th>Trial with Restitution Ordered</th></tr>
<tr><td>C2</td><td></td><td></td><td></td><td></td><td></td><td></td></tr>
<tr><td>C8</td><td></td><td></td><td></td><td></td><td></td><td></td></tr>
<tr><td>F3</td><td></td><td></td><td></td><td></td><td></td><td></td></tr>
<tr><td>F4</td><td></td><td></td><td></td><td></td><td></td><td></td></tr>
<tr><td>R5</td><td></td><td></td><td></td><td></td><td></td><td></td></tr>
<tr><td>R7</td><td></td><td></td><td></td><td></td><td></td><td></td></tr>
</table>

(Note that in the above table only certain case status' are included.)

Questions 61 - 75

61. Which two Judges had a total of 3 adjourned cases each during the three days?

A. Romano and Einfeld   C. Abram and Romano

B. Abram and Brendais   D. Brendais and Einfeld

62. What is the total number of cases for the three courts for the period Nov. 4, 2019 - November 8, 2019?

A. 33   C. 36

B. 35   D. none of the above

63. Which of the following Judges had a total of one adjourned case from Nov. 4, 2019 - November 8, 2019?
    A. Abram   C. Romano
    B. Baranov   D. none of the above

64. What is the total number of cases for the three courts that were filed in 2019?
    A. 18   C. 20
    B. 19   D. 21

65. How many Family Court cases were disposed by "Trial with restitution ordered"?
    A. 1   C. 4
    B. 3   D. 5

66. What is the total number of cases for the three courts that were filed in 2017 and 2018?
    A. 12   C. 13
    B. 14   D. 15

67. What is the total number of cases for the three courts that were defaulted or dismissed?
    A. 9   C. 7
    B. 10   D. 8

68. What is the total number of criminal cases that had a case status of something other than "Adjourned'?
    A. 7   C. 9
    B. 8   D. 10

69. What is the total number of "Dismissed" cases by Judges Brendais and Romano?
    A. 2   C. 4
    B. 3   D. 5

70. Which Judge had the greatest number of dismissed cases?
    A. Einfeld   C. Brendais
    B. Abram   D. Romano

71. The number of cases filed in 2019 exceeds the number of cases file in 2018 by what number?

A. 10   C. 12

B. 11   D. 13

72. Which of the following judges had a case that was "Defaulted"?

A. Baranov   C. Romano

B. Chin   D. Einfeld

73. Which of the following two Judges are Civil Court judges?

A. Chin and Romano   C. Brendais and Baranov

B. Einfeld and Barnov   D. Brendais and Abrams

74. What is the total number of Family Court cases and Criminal Court cases for the three days?.

A. 22   C. 24

B. 21   D. none of the above

75. The code "F3" is for which judge?

A. Brendais   C. Einfeld

B. Chin   D. none of the above

END OF QUESTIONS FOR PRACTICE TEST 1

ANSWERS: PRACTICE TEST 1

1. D. 9:00 a.m.	6. B. 3	11. C. six
2. C. Hastings	7. B. Franklin	12. B. Patterson
3. B. 21	8. D. Cavuto	13. C. Hastings
4. D. 11/14/2019	9. B. thirties	14. D. Franklin
5. C. Westbury	10. D. seventh	15. C. Nassau

16. d. precision (correct spelling)

17. c. slipping (logic of sentence)

18. d. terrorism (correct spelling)

19. b. problem (grammar: singular "problem" to agree with singular verb "is")

20. c. two (grammar: plural "two" to agree with plural "computer security programs")

21. c. enter (logic of sentence)

22. d. well lit (logic of sentence)

23. b. facility (correct spelling)

24. b. tall (logic of sentence)

25. d. ensure (vocabulary meaning; "make sure that something will occur.")

26. d. generated (logic of passage)

27. c. bronchitis (correct spelling)

28. d. have (to agree with plural "non-smokers")

29. b. exposed (vocabulary)

30. c. research (logic of sentence)

31. D. None of the above. (The procedure states that the person discovering the suspicious item should at first "Notify your facility supervisor, such as a manager, operator, or administrator, or follow your facility's standard operating procedure.")

32. D. Follow the Major's orders, wait for her Court Officer Supervisor and follow the supervisor's further directions. (The other choices are an overreach of authority and go against waiting for direction from the supervisor.)

33. D. He should inform his supervisor and note the missing clip-on mount in the Master BWC book. (step number 3 of the procedure)

34. B. Notify the man and the public that her BWC is recording (step 6 of the procedure).

35. D. Bring the malfunction to the attention of the Operations Office as soon as possible (step number 8 of the procedure).

36. A. Bail factors are defined in Civil Procedure Law Section 510.30. (This should read "...defined in **Criminal** Procedure Law Section 510.30".

37. C. the amount of bail is discretionary with the Judge.

38. C. the Judge

39. D. is scheduled for a court hearing.

40. D. are held every day

41. Choice A: if none of the three sets are exactly alike

    Weinford Ave. W. Weinford Ave. W.   Wein**fer**d Ave. W.

    ID: 73974-295389 ID: 73974-2953**98**   ID: 73974-295389

42. Choice D: if all the sets are exactly alike

43. Choice C: if only the first and second sets are exactly alike

    Rooms 17C and 22A Rooms 17C and 22A Rooms **17D** and 22A

44. Choice C: if only the first and second sets are exactly alike

    C: 28394-36886356 C: 28394-36886356 C: 28394-36886**536**

45. Choice B: if only the second and third sets are exactly alike

    Clerk Mary Rodrig**ues** Clerk Mary Rodriguez Clerk Mary Rodriguez

46. Choice A: if all the sets are exactly alike.

47. Choice D: if none of the three sets are exactly alike

    Report: SR2**825**EH   Report: SR2855EH   Report: SR2855EH

    Priority 7A, 8B, 9G   Priority 7A, 8B, 9G   Priority 7A, **88**, 9G

48. Choice C: if only the first and second sets are exactly alike

    Report Ref. 42G (h) Report Ref. 42G (h)   Report Ref. 42G **(n)**

49. Choice B: if only the second and third sets are exactly alike

    Vorliotis, Fran**cis**   Vorliotis, Frances   Vorliotis, Frances

50. Choice B: if only the second and third sets are exactly alike

    Sonya T. Aria**nof**   Sonya T. Arianoff   Sonya T. Arianoff

51. Choice C: if all the sets are exactly alike.

52. Choice A: if only the first and second sets are exactly alike

    Police Precinct 101   Police Precinct 101   Police Pre**cint** 101

53. Choice B: if only the second and third sets are exactly alike

    Diary 5**/18/**19 - 7/5/19   Diary 5/13/19 - 7/5/19 Diary 5/13/19 - 7/5/19

54. Choice D: if none of the three sets are exactly alike

    Mediator A. Mingano   Mediator A. M**img**ano   Mediator A. Ming**amo**

55. Choice A: if only the first and second sets are exactly alike

    254-397 Elder Street   254-397 Elder Street   254-397 El**dert** Street

56. Choice B: if only the first and second sets are exactly alike

    *Court Rep. Davidson   Court Rep. Davidson   Court Rep. Da**viso**n*

57. Choice B: if only the first and second sets are exactly alike

    Probated Section 13 Probated Section 13 Pro**bate** Section 13

58. Choice A: if only the second and third sets are exactly alike

    63581**314**7-62389 6358131147-62389 6358131147-62389

59. Choice C: if all the sets are exactly alike.

60. Choice B: if only the first and second sets are exactly alike

    Family Center 205 (b)   Family Center 205 (b)   Family Center **205 (d)**

Answers 61-75.

Summary Table 1:

Cases on Calendar November 4, 2019 - November 8, 2019				
Case Status	**Criminal**	**Family**	**Civil**	**Total Cases**
Adjourned	|||| 4	||| 3	||||| 5	12
Defaulted	| 1			1
Dismissed	||| 3	|||| 4	| 1	8
Settled - with Money Award			||| 3	3
Settled - no money award			|| 2	2
Trial with Fine Imposed	|| 2			2
Trial with no fine imposed	|| 2			2
Trial with Restitution Ordered		|||| 4		4
Trial with no Restitution Ordered		| 1		1
Total Cases	12	12	11	35
Cases by Date Filed				
2017	|| 2		|| 2	4
2018	|||| 4	||| 3	||| 3	10
2019	|||||| 6	||||| |||| 9	||||| | 6	21
Total Cases	12	12	11	35

Summary Table 2:

	Cases On Calendar					
	November 4, 2019 - November 8, 2019					
	Case Status at End of Day					
Part Code	Adjourned	Defaulted	Dismissed	Settled Money Award	Trial with Fine Imposed	Trial with Restitution Ordered
C2 Brendais	‖‖ 3			1		1		
C8 Abram	‖ 2			‖ 2		
F3 Chin		1			1			‖‖ 3
F4 Romano	‖ 2		‖‖ 3				1
R5 Einfeld	‖‖ 3		1		1			1	
R7 Baranov		1		‖ 2			1	

(Note that in the above table only certain case status' are included.)

61. D. Brendais and Einfeld

62. B. 35

63. B. Baranov

64. D. 21

65. C. 4

66. B. 14 (4 + 10)

67. A. 9 (1 + 8)

68. B. 8 (12 total - 4 adjourned = 8)

69. C. 4 (1 + 3 = 4)

70. D. Romano (3)

71. B. 11 (21 - 10 = 11)

72. D. Einfeld

73. D. Brendais and Abrams

74. C. 24 (12 + 12 = 24)

75. B. Chin

END OF ANSWERS FOR PRACTICE TEST 1

PRACTICE TEST 2: QUESTIONS

(75 Questions: Time allowed: 3.5 hours)

Questions 1-15: Remembering Facts and Information

"Directions: Read the brief story below. Study it for five minutes. Then, turn the story over and wait for ten minutes before you answer the fifteen questions on the following page. Try to remember as many details of the incident without making any written notes."*

(**Written test:** **At the end of the five minutes, the test monitor will collect this sheet and ten minutes after that, you will be instructed to begin the test by answering from memory the first fifteen questions relating to this story.**

Computer test: **At the end of the five minutes, the passage will disappear from the screen and ten minutes after that, you will be instructed to begin the test by answering from memory the first fifteen questions relating to this story.)**

On September 18, 2019, Court Officer-Trainee Beverly Madison was assigned to Civil Jury Part 15, located in room 407 of the Civil Court building at 25 Monroe Place in Nassau County. She was filling-in for the regularly assigned Court Officer, Susan Blanes, who had just started her two-week vacation.

Officer Madison reported to the part at 9:10 a.m. The Senior Court Clerk assigned to the part, Nicholas Daniken, introduced himself and informed Officer Madison that the judge had just given the case to the jury for the jurors to conduct their deliberations. All the six regular jurors were presently in the jury deliberations room, 407C, located next to the courtroom. Officer Madison assumed the security post at a desk in front of the jury deliberations room entrance.

At approximately 10:48 a.m., Officer Madison heard loud talking in the jury deliberations room, just before one of the female jurors opened the jury door and informed Officer Madison that one of the jurors was undergoing a possible heart seizure. Officer Madison rushed into the room and less than a minute later was on the radio, informing Court Officers headquarters on the fifth floor. Within minutes several other court officers arrived, including Court Officer-Sergeant Shaun Gallagher who was a certified medic. They stabilized the juror and within minutes after that, the medics from the responding ambulance arrived. Luckily, they determined that the juror was probably suffering from dehydration. However, they removed the juror by ambulance to County Hospital for further evaluation.

All the jurors and court staff were relieved that it was probably not a heart attack. Also, the jurors agreed to continue with the deliberations, with one of the alternate jurors replacing the juror who was now at the hospital. They reached a verdict in the afternoon, and by 3:30 p.m., the judge had thanked them and released them from the case.

Answer questions 1-15 on the following page based on the information provided in the preceding passage.

1. The jury reached a verdict _____.

A. at 12:49 p.m.   C. the next day

B. in the morning   D. in the afternoon

2. What is the date mentioned in the passage?

A. 7/19/2019   C. 9/18/2019

B. 9/9/2019   D. 9/8/2019

3. What is the number of the Civil Jury Part where Officer Madison was assigned?

A. 5   C. 25

B. 15   D. none of the above

4. At what time did Officer Madison report to the part?

A. 10:09 a.m.   C. 9:00 a.m.

B. 9:10 a.m.   D. none of the above

5. What is Officer Madison's first name?

A. Wavny   C. Beverly

B. Beatrice   D. Brenda

6. What was the title of the clerk assigned to the part?

A. Senior Court Clerk   C. Principal Court Clerk

B. Associate Court Clerk   D. Assistant Court Clerk

7. What is the room number of the jury deliberations room?

A. 407A   C. 407C

B. 407B   D. 407D

8. Court Officer Headquarters is on which floor?

A. second   C. fourth

B. third   D. fifth

9. By what time did the judge thank the jury and released them from the case?

A. 10:48 a.m.

B. 5:00 p.m.

C. 9:10 a.m.

D. 3:30 p.m.

10. What is the street address of the Civil Court building?

A. 25 Madison Plaza

B. 25 Monroe Place

C. 25 Madison Avenue

D. 25 Monroe Plaza

11. What is the last name of the court officer who is a certified medic?

A. Calloway

B. Gallagher

C. Galman

D. Gallego

12. The juror was taken to which hospital?

A. Cornelia Hospital

B. Cornwall Hospital

C. Kings Hospital

D. County Hospital

13. Officer Madison assumed the security post at _____ in front of the jury deliberations room entrance.

A. a booth

B. a kiosk

C. a desk

D. stanchion

14. The name of the Court Officer regularly assigned to the part is:

A. Susan Blame

B. Susan Blanes

C. Susan Blanner

D. Susan Blanton

15. At what time did Court Officer-Trainee Madison hear loud talking in the jury deliberations room?

A. 10:48 a.m.

B. 9:10 a.m.

C. 9:49 a.m.

D. 11:40 a.m.

▲

Questions 16 - 35 test for Reading, Understanding and Interpreting Written Material

"Directions: The three passages below each contain five numbered blanks. Below each passage are listed five sets of words numbered to match the blanks. Pick the word from each set which seems to make the most sense both in the sentence and the total paragraph."*

Passage 1

A ___16___ room or waiting hall is a building, or more commonly a part of a building or a room, where people sit or stand until the event or appointment for which they are waiting ___17___. There are ___18___ types of waiting rooms. One is where individuals leave for appointments one at a time, or in small groups, for instance at a doctor's office, a hospital triage area or outside a school headmaster's office. The other is where people leave en masse such as those at railway stations, bus stations, and airports. These two examples also highlight the difference between waiting rooms where one is asked to wait (private waiting rooms) and waiting rooms one can enter at will (___19___). People in private waiting rooms are queued up based on various methods in different types of waiting rooms. In hospital emergency department waiting areas, patients are ___20___ by a nurse, and they are seen by the doctor depending on the severity of their medical condition.(1)

16.	17.	18.	19.	20.
a. rest	a. commence	a. one	a. small	a. treaged
b. living	b. start	b. two	b. public	b. treeaged
c. waiting	c. ends	c. many	c. huge	c. treeged
d. outdoors	d. begins	d. single	d. private	d. triaged

Passage 2

___21___ trials are used in a significant share of serious criminal cases in many but not all common law judicial systems. The use of ___22___ trials, which evolved within common law systems rather than civil law systems, has had a ___23___ impact on the nature of American civil procedure and criminal procedure rules, even if a bench trial ___24___ actually contemplated in a particular case. In general, the availability of a jury trial if properly demanded has given rise to a system in which fact finding is concentrated in a single trial rather than multiple hearings, and appellate review of trial court decisions is greatly limited. Jury trials are of far ___25___ importance (or of no importance) in countries that do not have a common law system.(1)

21.	22.	23.	24.	25.
a. single	a. arbiter	a. proffound	a. were	a. more
b. epic	b. non-jury	b. profhound	b. is	b. less
c. quasi	c. jury	c. profound	c. were not	c. greater
d. jury	d. settled	d. proffund	d. weren't	d. much

Passage 3

Smoking bans are enacted in an attempt to protect people from the effects of second-hand ___26___, which include an increased risk of heart disease, cancer, emphysema, and other ___27___. Laws implementing bans on indoor smoking have been introduced by many countries in various forms over the ___28___, with some legislators citing scientific evidence that shows tobacco smoking is harmful to the smokers themselves and to those inhaling second-hand smoke. In addition such laws may ___29___ health care costs, improve work productivity, and lower the overall cost of labor in the community thus protected, making that workforce more attractive for employers. In the US state of Indiana, the economic development agency included in its 2006 plan for acceleration of economic ___30___ encouragement for cities and towns to adopt local smoking bans as a means of promoting job growth in communities.(1)

26.	27.	28.	29.	30.
a. air	a. excuses	a. day	a. increase	a. savings
b. smoke	b. thing	b. years	b. reduce	b. cuts
c. wind	c. diseases	c. week	c. balloon	c. growth
d. smoked	d. disesas	d. hour	d. jump	d. reduction

Questions 31- 35: Applying Facts and Information to Given Situations

"Directions: Use the information preceding each question to answer the question. Only that information should be used in answering the questions. Do not use any prior knowledge you may have on the subject. Choose the alternative that best answers the question."*

Questions 31 and 32 refer to the following Rule:

Rules for Part 16

Judge Ellerman, the Judge presiding in Part 16, has promulgated the following evidence exhibits rules for the Part:

1. All exhibits entered into evidence shall be marked with a sequential exhibit number by the Court Reporter in the part.
2. The Clerk of the part shall maintain an exhibits log.
3. The Court Officer in the part shall secure the exhibits in a locked cabinet in the Part.
4. Viewing of the exhibits before or after the daily trial session by any party shall only be allowed upon the written order of the Judge Ellerman.
5. Exhibits used during a trial shall be under the direct supervision of the Court Officer.
6. Exhibits other than paper documents shall be stored in the central exhibit storage room, 407.

Situation for question 31 and 32

During a jury trial in Part 16 (Judge Ellerman), relating to an auto accident, a defective seat belt is allowed into evidence by Judge Ellerman.

31. Based on the above rules and situation, which of the following statements relating to the seat belt is not correct?

A. The Court Reporter marks the seat belt exhibit entered into evidence with a sequential exhibit number.

B. The Court Officer secures exhibits in the Part.

C. Exhibits can be viewed after a daily session if the Judge orders it in writing.

D. The seat belt must be secured by the Court Officer in the Part and stored in a locked cabinet in the Part.

32. Based on the preceding rules and situation, which of the following statements is not correct?

A. The Court Officer maintains supervision of exhibits during trial.

B. The exhibits log is maintained by the Clerk of the Part.

C. Paper document exhibits are not stored in room 407.

D. The rules cannot be applied to seat belts exhibits.

Questions 33 - 35 are based on the following Magnetometer Procedure

Magnetometer Procedure

Every entrance to the criminal court building must have at least one magnetometer station and one X-ray machine, each staffed by a minimum of two Court Officers. All member of the public must pass through the magnetometer station and all packages and clothing not worn on the person must be scanned through the X-ray machine.

The following are not required to pass through the magnetometer station and may enter through the "Open Security Gate."

1. Judges and court personnel with current NYS Courts ID security card.

2. Police officers and NYS peace officers.

3. Attorneys with a valid CSC ID security card.

4. Emergency personnel from municipal departments.

5. Persons waived through by a Court Officer Captain or Court Officer Major.

If a firearm is suspected of not being registered, the firearm must be seized and the Captain or Major informed immediately so that they can attend to the matter. The Court Officer who seized the suspected illegal firearm is required to complete for IR-1 and submit it to Building Headquarters prior to the end of the Court Officer's shift. All legal firearms must be secured in the Central Security Safe located in room 201. An FSR1 form must be completed in duplicate for each firearm. The original is logged into the DFSL book and then placed with the firearm into the Central Security Safe. At any time during the day, the owner of the firearm as he is leaving the court building, may present his FSR1 form and retrieve the firearm. Any unusual material circumstances that arise and that are not stated in the above procedure should be immediately brought to the attention of the Court Officer Major.

Question 33 situation

You are a Court Officer assigned to Magnetometer Station 1 on the first floor of the criminal court building. You notice that a person on the magnetometer line has a 45 caliber handgun that is slightly showing in his pants pocket.

33. According to the preceding procedure and situation, which of the following choices is the best action for you to take?

A. Arrest the person for possession of a firearm.

B. Immediately notify the Court Officer Major.

C. Determine if the firearm is registered, and if so, secure it in the Central Security Safe.

D. None of the above

Question 34 situation

At the morning roster call, you are assigned to Magnetometer station 4 at the rear entrance of the criminal court building. This entrance is used infrequently. It is connected to an ADA ramp and used mainly by persons with disabilities. When you arrive at the magnetometer station, you receive a radio message by the other Court Officer assigned to the magnetometer station that she is in the process of detaining a suspected drug dealer and that she will not be able to report to the magnetometer station for about two hours.

34. According to the preceding procedure and situation, what is the best first action that you should take?

A. You should return to the locker room until a second Court Officer is assigned.

B. Close the entrance immediately for security reasons.

C. Operate the magnetometer station as well as you can without the second Court Officer.

D. Inform the Court Officer Major of the need for a second Court Officer for the magnetometer station.

Question 35 situation

You are a Court Officer assigned to Magnetometer Station 3 on the first floor. Attorney Jack Higgins, who handles one or two cases a week at this court, informs you that he has forgotten his CSC ID card at home, but that his assistant will be coming with it in about half an hour. Because he is late to his calendar call in Part 17, he asks that you do him the courtesy of letting him pass through without having to wait on the long Magnetometer Station line.

35. According to the preceding procedure and situation, what is the best first action that you should take?

A. Let Jack Higgins pass through without having to wait on the long Magnetometer Station line because he is an attorney.

B. Let Attorney Jack Higgins through without having to wait on the long Magnetometer Station line because his assistant will be coming with the CSC ID security card.

C. Let Attorney Jack Higgins through without having to wait on the Magnetometer Station line because the line is very long.

D. Inform the attorney that he must wait in line and pass through the magnetometer station.

For questions 36 - 40, read the passage and then answer the questions based solely on the information provided in the passage.

Passage for questions 36-37

First aid is the first and immediate assistance given to any person suffering from either a minor or serious illness or injury, with care provided to preserve life, prevent the condition from worsening, or to promote recovery. It includes initial intervention in a serious condition prior to professional medical help being available, such as performing cardiopulmonary resuscitation (CPR) while waiting for an ambulance, as well as the complete treatment of minor conditions, such as applying a plaster to a cut. First aid is generally performed by someone with basic medical training. Mental health first aid is an extension of the concept of first aid to cover mental health, while psychological first aid is used as early treatment of people at risk for developing PTSD. There are many situations which may require first aid, and many countries have legislation, regulation, or guidance which specifies a minimum level of first aid provision in certain circumstances. This can include specific training or equipment to be available in the workplace (such as an automated external defibrillator), the provision of specialist first aid cover at public gatherings, or mandatory first aid training within schools. First aid, however, does not necessarily require any particular equipment or prior knowledge, and can involve improvisation with materials available at the time, often by untrained people. (1)

36. Which of the following statements is supported by the above passage?

A. First aid is always performed by someone with basic medical training.

B. The performance of cardiopulmonary resuscitation (CPR) is not included in first aid.

C. First aid requires that a trained person administers it.

D. An automated external defibrillator is required by certain countries to be available.

37. In the above passage, PTSD is described as:

A. Prior Treatment for Serious Disease

B. Post Treatment for Serious Disease

C. Preliminary Treatment for Serious Disease

D. none of the above

Passage for question 38

Procedural law, adjective law, in some jurisdictions referred to as remedial law, or rules of court comprises the rules by which a court hears and determines what happens in civil, lawsuit, criminal or administrative proceedings. The rules are designed to ensure a fair and consistent application of due process (in the U.S.) or fundamental justice (in other common law countries) to all cases that come before a court. Substantive law, which refers to the actual claim and defense whose validity is tested through the procedures of procedural law, is different from procedural law. In the context of procedural law, procedural rights may also refer not exhaustively to rights to information, access to justice, and rights to public participation, with those rights encompassing, general civil and political rights. (1)

38. Which of the following statements is supported by the preceding passage?

A. Adjective law and remedial law refer to two different types of laws.

B. Procedural law is sometimes referred to as substantive law.

C. Due process is the aim of substantive law.

D. Procedural law refers to rules of court.

Passage for questions 39-40

The practical authority given to the court is known as its jurisdiction – the court's power to decide certain kinds of questions or petitions put to it. According to William Blackstone's Commentaries on the Laws of England, a court is constituted by a minimum of three parties: the actor or plaintiff, who complains of an injury done; the reus or defendant, who is called upon to make satisfaction for it, and the judex or judicial power, which is to examine the truth of the fact, to determine the law arising upon that fact, and, if any injury appears to have been done, to ascertain and by its officers to apply a legal remedy. It is also usual in the superior courts to have barristers, and attorneys or counsel, as assistants, though, often, courts consist of additional barristers, bailiffs, reporters, and perhaps a jury. The term "the court" is also used to refer to the presiding officer or officials, usually one or more judges. The judge or panel of judges may also be collectively referred to as "the bench" (in contrast to attorneys and barristers, collectively referred to as "the bar"). In the United States, and other common law jurisdictions, the term "court" (in the case of U.S. federal courts) by law is used to describe the judge himself or herself. In the United States, the legal authority of a court to take action is based on personal jurisdiction over the parties to the litigation and subject-matter jurisdiction over the claims asserted.(1)

39. Which of the following statements is not supported by the preceding passage?

A. "Jurisdiction" is the practical authority given to the court.

B. The "Commentaries on the Laws of England" were authored by William Blackstone.

C. The term "the court" is also used to refer to the plaintiff.

D. none of the above

40. According to the above passage, a court is constituted by:

A. claimant, defendant, judicial power

B. plaintiff, respondent and judex

C. a plaintiff, reus, and judicial power

D. none of the above

▲

Questions 41-60: Clerical Checking

Directions: The following example consists of five sets of information. Compare the information in the three sets, and on your answer sheet, mark:

Choice A: if none of the three sets are exactly alike

Choice B: if only the second and third sets are exactly alike

Choice C: if only the first and second sets are exactly alike

Choice D: if all the sets are exactly alike

41. Referee M. Simpson MHL 90.21 (a - c) 3289-21 2nd Avenue Records 2019: S3287 H. Harry Weinerstein	41. Referee M. Simpson MHL 90.21 (a - c) 3289-21 2nd Avenue Records 2019: S3287 H. Harry Weinerstein	41. Referee M. Simpson MHL 90.21 (a - c) 3289-21 2nd Avenue Record 2019: S3287 *H. Harry Weinerstein*
42. DEF: 4/18/19 - K-M 3893 West Elm St. Ct. Reporter Burnett Massawa, PA 11395	42. DEF: 4/18/19 - K-M **3893 West Elm St.** Ct. Reporter Burnett Massawa, PA 11395	42. DEF: 4/18/19 - K-M 3893 West Elm St. Ct. Reporter Burnett Massawa, PA 11395
43. SCPA 324 N. 427.19 *Kerry Kerns, JHO* SGT 3755/2020 7/2 J. Volker - Ref. 2653	43. SCPA 324 N. 427.19 Kerry Kerns, JHO SGT 3755/2020 7/2 J. Volker - Ref. 2653	43. SCPA 324 N. 427.19 Kerry Kerns, JHO SGT 3725/2020 7/2 J. Volker - Ref. 2653
44. Dewey and Liverton **371283862-869499** 862-875-3179 (NC) CPLR 1001 (a - z)	44. Dewey and Liverton 371283862-869499 862-875-3179 (NC) CPLR 1001 (a - z)	44. Dewy and Liverton 371283862-869499 862-875-3179 (NC) CPLR 1001 (a - z)
45. Marietta N. Luima Support Magistrate CA Georgina Baynes Mona Susan Wiener	45. Marietta N. Luima Support Magistrate CA Georgina Baynes Mona Susan Weiner	45. **Marietta N. Luima** Support Magistrate CA Georgina Baynes Mona Susan Weiner

Court Officer-Trainee: 5 Full Practice Exams for 2020

Directions: The following example consists of five sets of information. Compare the information in the three sets, and on your answer sheet, mark:

Choice A: if all the sets are exactly alike

Choice B: if only the second and third sets are exactly alike

Choice C: if only the first and second sets are exactly alike

Choice D: if none of the three sets are exactly alike

46. JHO Barney Lehman SCPA Amend. 27-20 **Permit B8JH69MH** Dinkins, Frederick	46. JHO Barney Lehman SCPA Amend. 27-20 Permit B8JH69MH *Dinkins, Frederick*	46. JHO Barney Lehman SPCA Amend. 27-20 Permit B8JH69MH Dinkins, Frederick
47. TLOC 25K 7/2019 3862 Minster Avenue Section 3763-39736 Fall & Becker, PC	47. TLOC 25K 7/2019 3862 Minster Avenue Section 3763-39736 Falls & Becker, PC	47. TLOC 25K 7/2019 3862 Minster Avenue Section 3763-39736 Falls & Becker, PC
48. Kingston Blvd., West Files 48591-49859 4/8/2019, 5/28/19 INT. Susan Morales	48. Kingston Blvd., West Files 48591-49859 4/8/2019, 5/28/19 INT. Susan Morales	48. Kingston Blvd., West Files 48591-49859 4/8/2019, 5/28/19 **INT. Susan Morales**
49. Parts 24A, 28C, 30A *Examiner Hernadez* Albany and Oswego Five Fingers area	49. Parts 24A, 28C, 30A Examiner Hernadez Albany and Oswego Five Finger area	49. Parts 24A, 28C, 30A Examiner Hernandez Albany and Oswego Five Fingers area
50. NYCFD Section E-5 Cisco Rodriguex Ref. Numb. 558914 Civil File A-78862/19	50. NYCFD Section E-5 **Cisco Rodriguex** Ref. Numb. 558914 Civil File A-78862/19	50. NYCFD Section E-5 Cisco Rodriguex Ref. Numb. 559814 Civil File A-78862/19

Directions: The following example consists of five sets of information. Compare the information in the three sets, and on your answer sheet, mark:

Choice A: if only the first and second sets are exactly alike

Choice B: if only the second and third sets are exactly alike

Choice C: if all the sets are exactly alike.

Choice D: if none of the three sets are exactly alike

51. Magistrate Davidson *VTL Amend. 48-21* License C8KN89N Boris R. Kuznetsov	51. Magistrate Davidson VTL Amend. 48-21 License C8KN89N Boris R. Kuznetsov	51. Magistrate Davidson VTL Amend. 48-21 License C8KN39N Boris R. Kuznetsov
52. Part 19 (3/29/2020) 3492 S. Kingbridge Section 4725-17637 Ivanov & Brand, PC	52. Part 19 (3/29/2020) **3492 S. Kingsbridge** Section 4725-17637 Ivanov & Brand, PC	52. Part 19 (3/29/2020) 3492 S. Kingsbridge *Section 4725-17637* Ivanov & Brand, PC
53. Gosmar Blvd., West Files 38697-499172 5/11/2019, 6/29/19 Maj. Benjamin Verner	53. Gosmar Blvd., West Files 38697-499172 *5/11/2019, 6/29/19* Maj. Benjamin Verner	53. Gosmar Blvd., West Files 38697-499172 5/11/2019, 6/29/19 Maj. Benjamin Verner
54. Parts 32M, 17C, 17B Referee James Chen Otsego, Westchester 568-275-3629 Ext. 9	54. Parts 32M, 17C, 17B Referee James Chen Otswego, Westchester 568-275-3629 Ext. 9	54. Parts 32M, 17C, 17B Referee James Chan Otsego, Westchester **568-275-3629 Ext. 9**
55. Suffolk Section 2465 Vanessa L. Zhang **Ref. Numb. 256662** FC File P-28764/20	55. Suffolk Section 2465 Vanessa L. Zhang Ref. Numb. 256662 FC File P-28764/20	55. Suffolk Section 2465 Vanessa L. Zhang Ref. Numb. 256662 FC File P-28164/20

Directions: The following example consists of five sets of information. Compare the information in the three sets, and on your answer sheet, mark:

Choice A: if only the second and third sets are exactly alike

Choice B: if only the first and second sets are exactly alike

Choice C: if all the sets are exactly alike

Choice D: if none of the three sets are exactly alike

56. Witness Ted Kamiski VTL Amend. 46-20 License KJA3J79M Barnaby, William	56. Witness Ted Kamiski VTL Amend. 46-20 License KJA3J79M Barnaby, William	56. Witness Ted Kamiski **VTL Amend. 46-20** License KJA3J79M Barnaby, William
57. *Parts 19A and 21P 9)* 4831 Southern Pkwy. Sect. NF6341: 57817 Stamos & Dean, PC	57. Parts 19A and 21P 9) 4813 Southern Pkwy. Sect. NF6341: 57817 Stamos & Dean, PC	57. Parts 19A and 21P 9) *4831 Southern Pkwy.* Sect. NF6341: 57817 Stamos & Doan, PC
58. (1) 719-398-2798 **Files 68992-49834** 7/9/2419, 8/22/19 COT Belinda Movers	58. (1) 719-398-2798 Files 68992-49834 7/9/2419, 8/22/19 COT Belinda Movers	58. (1) 719-398-2798 Files 68992-49834 7/9/2419, 8/22/19 COT Bellinda Movers
59. 4828 East 19th Ave. Expert Witness es Family or Criminal Ct. Priority Calendar 5	59. 4828 East 19th Ave. *Expert Witness es* Family or Criminal Ct. Priority Calendar 5	59. 4828 East 16th Ave. Expert Witness es **Family or Criminal Ct.** Priority Calendar 5
60. Thursday Special Crim. docket S-9578 Williamburg cases Locations D1-D19	60. Thursday Special Crim. docket S-9578 Williamsburg cases Locations D1-D19	60. Thursday Special Crim. docket S-9578 Williamsburg cases Locations D1-D19

Questions 61-75: Record Keeping

"Directions: Answer the fifteen questions based on the information contained in the following tables. Remember, all of the information needed to answer the questions correctly can be found in the tables. Complete the "Daily Breakdown of Cases" and "Summary of Cases" tables before you attempt to answer any of the questions."*

"Part" means Courtroom

"Date Filed" is date the first papers of the case were filed with the clerk of the court.

"Status" means the status of the case at the end of the court session.

"Money Award" means the amount of money that was awarded on that case. The money is usually awarded to the party seeking money damages and is paid by the party who was sued.

Daily List of Cases Monday			Table 1
Part	**Date Filed**	**Status of Case**	**Money Award**
Part 20	02/11/17	Settled	$ 7,400
Part 18	09/03/18	Adjourned	X
Part 19	03/08/17	Dismissed	X
Part 17	06/21/18	Settled	X
Part 18	07/14/18	Adjourned	X
Part 20	09/04/18	Dismissed	X
Part 19	11/11/18	Adjourned	X
Part 17	11/13/18	Settled	$ 12,600
Part 18	02/12/19	Defaulted	X
Part 17	05/25/19	Adjourned	X
Part 20	07/10/19	Settled	$ 11,900
Part 17	09/26/19	Dismissed	X
Part 19	11/06/19	Settled	X

Daily List of Cases Tuesday			Table 2
Part	**Date Filed**	**Status of Case**	**Money Award**
Part 19	06/05/17	Dismissed	X
Part 17	09/09/17	Settled	$ 16,800
Part 20	07/11/17	Adjourned	X
Part 18	08/29/17	Settled	X
Part 19	01/16/18	Dismissed	X
Part 20	03/08/18	Dismissed	X
Part 18	06/24/18	Adjourned	X
Part 20	07/19/18	Settled	$ 14,700
Part 17	12/17/18	Adjourned	X
Part 19	02/21/19	Settled	$ 13,900
Part 18	04/17/19	Dismissed	X
Part 17	05/28/19	Defaulted	X
Part 18	07/13/19	Defaulted	X
Part 19	08/19/19	Settled	$ 19,500
Part 17	10/12/19	Adjourned	X
Part 20	12/13/19	Settled	X

Daily List of Cases Wednesday			Table 3
Part	**Date Filed**	**Status of Case**	**Money Award**
Part 18	08/14/17	Adjourned	X
Part 20	01/05/17	Settled	$ 14,700
Part 19	10/13/17	Defaulted	X
Part 17	05/29/17	Settled	X
Part 18	07/16/18	Adjourned	X
Part 19	09/11/18	Dismissed	X
Part 19	09/17/18	Dismissed	X
Part 20	11/29/18	Settled	$17,500
Part 17	12/15/18	Adjourned	X
Part 19	01/22/19	Dismissed	X
Part 19	03/16/19	Settled	$ 18,900
Part 20	05/21/19	Defaulted	X
Part 17	07/27/19	Settled	$ 13,800
Part 18	08/07/19	Dismissed	X
Part 17	09/16/19	Defaulted	X
Part 18	11/07/19	Adjourned	X

				Table 4
Daily Analysis of Cases: Monday, Tuesday, Wednesday				
Status of Case	**Monday**	**Tuesday**	**Wednesday**	**Total Cases**
Adjourned				
Defaulted				
Dismissed				
Settled - with Money Award				
Settled- with No Money Award				
Total Cases				
Cases by Year Filed				
2017				
2018				
2019				
Total Cases				

Table 5: Summary of Cases from Monday, Tuesday, Wednesday					
	Case Status at End of Day				
Part	**Adjourned**	**Defaulted**	**Dismissed**	**Settled With Money Award**	**Settled No Money Award**	**Total Cases**
17						
18						
19						
20						

Questions 61-75

61. What is the total number of "Adjourned" cases for all four parts for Monday through Wednesday?
   A. 10   C. 12
   B. 11   D. 13

62. What is the total number of cases for all parts for Mon. - Wed. that were filed in 2018?
   A. 15   C. 14
   B. 17   D. none of the above

63. What is the total number of cases that were "Settled - with Money Award" for the three days?
   A. 10   C. 12
   B. 11   D. none of the above

64. Which part had the greatest number of cases "Settled With Money Award?"
   A. Part 17   C. Part 20
   B. Part 19   D. none of the above

65. The total number of adjourned cases for all the parts exceeds the total number of defaulted cases for all parts by_____.
   A. 3   C. 5
   B. 4   D. 6

66. Which day had the greatest number of cases that were filed in 2018?
   A. Monday   C. Wednesday
   B. Tuesday   D. None. There was a tie.

67. What is the total number of "adjourned" cases plus "dismissed" cases for the three days?
   A. 21   C. 24
   B. 22   D. 23

68. What is the number of cases that appeared on the calendar on Tuesday that were not filed in 2017?
   A. 10   C. 13
   B. 12   D. 9

69. What is the total number of case "Settled - with Money Award" plus cases "Settled - with No Money Award?"

   A. 14   C. 15

   B. 17   D. 16

70. What is the total number of cases filed in 2017 and 2019?

   A. 28   C. 29

   B. 31   D. 30

71. Which part handled the greatest number of cases that were "adjourned?

   A.19   C. 18

   B. 17   D. 20

72. Which two parts had the same number of "Settled With Money Award" for the three days.

   A. Parts 19 and 20   C. Parts 18 and 19

   B. Parts 17 and 19   D. none of the above

73. How many cases were filed in 2019?

   A. 18   C. 17

   B. 19   D. none of the above

74. What is the total number of cases dismissed in Part 19?

   A. 3   C. 5

   B. 4   D. 6

75. The total number of cases that were not dismissed is___.

   A. 36   C. 37

   B. 34   D. 35

END OF QUESTIONS FOR PRACTICE TEST 2

ANSWERS: PRACTICE TEST 2

1. D. in the afternoon	6. A. Senior Court Clerk	11. B. Gallaher
2. C. 9/18/2019	7. C. 407C	12. D. County Hospital
3. B. 15	8. D. fifth	13. C. a desk
4. B. 9:10 a.m.	9. D. 3:30 p.m.	14. B. Susan Blanes
5. C. Beverly	10. B. 25 Monroe Place	15. A. 10:48 a.m.

16. C. waiting (logic, agreement with rest of paragraph)

17. D. begins (singular to agree with singular "event" or "appointment")

18. B. two (agreement with two types of rooms mentioned later)

19. B. public (logic)

20. D. triaged (spelling)

21. D. jury (subject of passage)

22. C. jury (again, subject of passage)

23. C. profound (spelling)

24. B. is (grammar, singular - to agree with "a bench trial") and present tense

25. B. less (agreement with logic of passage)

26. B. smoke (subject of passage)

27. C. diseases (logic)

28. B. years (logic and plural)

29. B. reduce (logic)

30. C. growth (logic)

31. D. The seat belt must be secured by the Court Officer in the Part and stored in a locked cabinet in the Part. (This statement is not correct because the exhibit must be stored in room 407.)

32. D. The rules cannot be applied to seat belts exhibits. (This is the answer because this statement is not correct. The rules apply to seat belts: "6. Exhibits other than paper documents shall be stored in the central exhibit storage room, 407.")

33. C. Determine if the firearm is registered, and if so, secure it in the Central Security Safe. The Magnetometer Procedure (Number 5) states, "All legal firearms must be secured in the Central Security Safe located in room 201...."

34. D. Inform the Court Officer Major of the need for a second Court Officer for the magnetometer

station. The Magnetometer Procedure states, "Any unusual material circumstances that arise and that are not stated in the above procedure should be immediately brought to the attention of the Court Officer Major."

35. D. Inform the attorney that he must wait in line and pass through the magnetometer station. ("The following are not required to pass through the magnetometer station and may enter through the "Open Security Gate...Attorneys with a valid CSC ID security card."

36. D. An automated external defibrillator is required by certain countries to be available. ("This can include specific training or equipment to be available in the workplace (such as an automated external defibrillator), the provision of specialist first aid cover at public gatherings, or mandatory first aid training within schools.")

37. D. none of the above

38. D. Procedural law refers to rules of court.

39. C. The term "the court" is also used to refer to the plaintiff. ("The term "the court" is also used to refer to the presiding officer or officials, usually one or more judges.")

40. C. a plaintiff, reus, and judicial power ("...a court is constituted by a minimum of three parties: the actor or plaintiff, who complains of an injury done; the reus or defendant, who is called upon to make satisfaction for it, and the judex or judicial power....")

41. Choice C: if only the first and second sets are exactly alike
    Records 2019: S3287   Records 2019: S3287   Rec**ord** 2019: S3287

42. Choice D: if all the sets are exactly alike

43. Choice C: if only the first and second sets are exactly alike
    SGT 3755/2020 7/2   SGT 3755/2020 7/2   SGT 37**25**/2020 7/2

44. Choice C: if only the first and second sets are exactly alike
    Dewey and Liverton   Dewey and Liverton   D**ewy** and Liverton

45. Choice B: if only the second and third sets are exactly alike
    Mona Susan W**ie**ner   Mona Susan Weiner   Mona Susan Weiner

46. Choice C: if only the first and second sets are exactly alike
    SCPA Amend. 27-20   SCPA Amend. 27-20   **SPCA** Amend. 27-20

47. Choice B: if only the second and third sets are exactly alike
    Fall & Becker, PC   Falls & Becker, PC   Falls & Becker, PC

48. Choice A: if all the sets are exactly alike

49. Choice D: if none of the three sets are exactly alike
    Examiner Hernadez   Examiner Hernadez   Examiner Hern**and**ez
    Fingers are   Fi**nger** area   Fingers area

50. Choice C: if only the first and second sets are exactly alike

   Ref. Numb. 558914   Ref. Numb. 558914   Ref. Numb. 55**98**14

51. Choice A: if only the first and second sets are exactly alike

   License C8KN89N   License C8KN89N   License C8KN**39**N

52. Choice B: if only the second and third sets are exactly alike

   3492 S. Ki**ngbr**idge   3492 S. Kingsbridge   3492 S. Kingsbridge

53. Choice C: if all the sets are exactly alike.

54. Choice D: if none of the three sets are exactly alike

   Referee James Chen   Referee James Chen   Referee James **Chan**

   Otsego, Westchester Ot**swe**go, Westchester Otsego, Westchester

55. Choice A: if only the first and second sets are exactly alike

   FC File P-28764/20 FC File P-28764/20   FC File P-2**816**4/20

56. Choice C: if all the sets are exactly alike

57. Choice D: if none of the three sets are exactly alike

   4831 Southern Pkwy.   4**813** Southern Pkwy.   4831 Southern Pkwy.

   Stamos & Dean, PC   Stamos & Dean, PC   Stamos & **Doan**, PC

58. Choice B: if only the first and second sets are exactly alike

   COT Belinda Movers   COT Belinda Movers   COT B**ellin**da Movers

59. Choice B: if only the first and second sets are exactly alike

   4828 East 19th Ave.   4828 East 19th Ave.   4828 East **16th** Ave.

60. Choice A: if only the second and third sets are exactly alike

   Willi**amb**urg cases   Williamsburg cases   Williamsburg cases

Table 4: Daily Analysis of Cases: Monday, Tuesday, Wednesday

Status of Case	Monday		Tuesday		Wednesday		Total Cases
Adjourned	||||	4	||||	4	||||	4	12
Defaulted	|	1	||	2	|||	3	6
Dismissed	|||	3	||||	4	||||	4	11
Settled - with Money Award	|||	3	||||	4	||||	4	11
Settled- with No Money Award	||	2	||	2	|	1	5
Total Cases		13		16		16	45
Cases by Year Filed							
2017	||	2	||||	4	||||	4	10
2018	||||||	6	|||||	5	|||||	5	16
2019	|||||	5	|||| ||	7	|||| ||	7	19
Total Cases		13		16		16	45

Table 5: Summary of Cases from Monday, Tuesday, Wednesday

Part	Case Status at End of Day					Total Cases
	Adjourned	Defaulted	Dismissed	Settled With Money Award	Settled No Money Award	
17	|||| 4	|| 2	| 1	||| 3	|| 2	12
18	||||| | 6	|| 2	|| 2		| 1	11
19	| 1	| 1	||||| | 6	||| 3	| 1	12
20	| 1	| 1	|| 2	||||| 5	| 1	10
	12	6	11	11	5	45

61. C. 12

62. D. none of the above (Correct number of cases is 16.)

63. B. 11

64. C. Part 20 (5 cases)

65. D. 6 (12 - 6 = 6)

66. A. Monday (6)

67. D. 23 (12 + 11 = 23)

68. B. 12 (16 - 4 = 12)

69. D. 16 (11 + 5 = 16)

70. C. 29 (10 + 19 = 29)

71. C. 18

72. B. Parts 17 and 19 (3 each)

73. B. 19

74. D. 6

75. B. 34 (45 - 11 = 34)

END OF ANSWERS FOR PRACTICE TEST 2

PRACTICE TEST 3: QUESTIONS

(75 Questions: Time allowed: 3.5 hours)

Questions 1-15: Remembering Facts and Information

"Directions: Read the brief story below. Study it for five minutes. Then, turn the story over and wait for ten minutes before you answer the fifteen questions on the following page. Try to remember as many details of the incident without making any written notes."*

(Written test: At the end of the five minutes, the test monitor will collect this sheet and ten minutes after that, you will be instructed to begin the test by answering from memory the first fifteen questions relating to this story.

Computer test: At the end of the five minutes, the passage will disappear from the screen and ten minutes after that, you will be instructed to begin the test by answering from memory the first fifteen questions relating to this story.)

On Tuesday, November 5, 2019, a report from the New York Police Department was received by the Court Officers' Headquarters at the criminal court in Queens county. The report was in the form of an email and contained specifics about a demonstration that was planned for the following day. The "Warriors for Justice", a radical group that opposed any type of incarceration, was organizing approximately two hundred of their followers to picket the entrance of the criminal court building at the corner of Connors Avenue and Beltway Street. Their declared purpose was to disrupt the trial of one of their members, a suspected arsonist, that was scheduled for 9:30 a.m., in Part 16 on the fourth floor.

Upon receiving the report, Major Martinez informed Supervising Judge Eleanor Grant, the Judge in the Part, Judge Deborah Massing, and Chief Clerk Arnold Powell. Together they determined that an extra court officer for the part was warranted and that the outside perimeter security detail would be increased from two court officers to six. In addition, all court officers in the building were instructed to wear full emergency gear and be ready for any situation that might arise.

On Wednesday morning, at 8:00 a.m., approximately two hundred fifty members of the group surrounded the main entrance. Court Officers were successful in clearing the entrance. However, one of the demonstrators who was wearing a T-shirt with the logo "Anarchy Forever", pulled out two pairs of handcuffs and handcuffed his wrists to the entrance poor, thereby preventing anyone from entering the court building. Major Martinez contacted Headquarters by radio and then cleared the area around the protestor. He spoke to the protestor and managed to keep the protestor and his two hundred-fifty companions calm for a few minutes, until Sergeant Foster appeared with a large set of bolt cutters. Within minutes after that, the protester was in custody. The other protesters were informed that they had a choice between protesting peacefully or facing   arrest. They chose to protest peacefully, and the trial of their group member proceeded without any further disturbance.

Answer questions 1-15 based on the information provided in the passage which you have read.

1. In which county does the preceding incidents occur?

A. Kings County   C. New York County

B. Suffolk County   D. Queens County

2. At 8:00 a.m., approximately how many members of the group surrounded the main entrance?

A. one hundred fifty   C. three hundred fifty

B. two hundred fifty   D. none of the above

3. What is the name of the radical group?

A. War on Justice   C. Justice League

B. Warriors for Justice   D. Justice Warriors

4. What was the protestor wearing that had the logo "Anarchy Forever" on it?

A. T-shirt   C. polo shirt

B. sweat shirt   D. none of the above

5. What did the protester handcuff to the entrance door?

A. arms   C. wrists

B. legs   D. none of the above

6. What is the part number where the trial of the suspected arsonist was scheduled?

A. Part 14   C. Part 19

B. Part 16   D. none of the above

7. On what floor was the trial of the suspected arsonist scheduled?

A. first floor   C. third floor

B. second floor   D. fourth floor

8. The incidents in the preceding passage occurred on what date?

A. September 5, 2018   C. November 5, 2019

B. November 5, 2018   D. September 5, 2019

9. What is the name of the supervising judge?

A. Eleanor Grant   C. Ellen Powell

B. Ellen Grant   D. Eleanor Powell

10. What is the name of the Chief Clerk?

A. Arnold Grant   C. Ellen Powell

B. Ellen Grant   D. Arnold Powell

11. What is the last name of the Major?

A. Rodriguez   C. Ramirez

B. Hernandez   D. Martinez

12. What is the name of the officer who brought the bolt cutters?

A. Sergeant Foster   C. Captain Powell

B. Major Ramirez   D. Sergeant Fuller

13. The report from the New York Police Department was in what form?

A. express mail   C. phone call

B. email   D. phone text message

14. The trial of the suspected arsonist was scheduled for what time?

A. 9:30 a.m.   C. 10:00 a.m.

B. 9:45 a.m.   D. 10:30 a.m.

15. The entrance of the criminal court building is at the corner of Connors Avenue and which street?

A. Bellway Street   C. Beltway Street

B. Belford Street   D. Belfast Street

▲

Questions 16-30: Reading, Understanding and Interpreting Written Material

"Directions: The three passages below each contain five numbered blanks. Below each passage are listed five sets of words numbered to match the blanks. Pick the word from each set which seems to make the most sense both in the sentence and the total paragraph."*

Passage 1 (Questions 16 - 20)

Public service ___16___ a service purporting to serve all members of a community. It is usually provided by government to people living within its ___17___, either directly (through the public sector) or by financing provision of services. The term is associated with a social consensus (usually expressed through ___18___ elections) that certain services should be available to all, regardless of income, physical ability or mental ___19___. Even where public services are neither publicly provided nor publicly financed, for social and political reasons they are usually subject to regulation going beyond that applying to most economic sectors. Public policy when made in the public's interest and motivations can provide public services. Public service is also a course that can be studied at a college or ___20___. Examples of public services are the fire brigade, police, air force, and paramedics. (1)

16.	17.	18.	19.	20.
a. was	a. jurysprudence	a. demographic	a. accuiti	a. pre-k
b. is	b. juryprudence	b. democratic	b. acuiti	b. university
c. isn't	c. jurisprudence	c. democracy	c. akuity	c. shop
d. wasn't	d. jurisdiction	d. belated	d. acuity	d. junior high

Passage 2 (Questions 21 - 30)

A court of record is a trial court or appellate court in which a ___21___ of the proceedings is captured and ___22___, for the possibility of appeal. A court clerk or a court reporter takes down a record of ___23___ proceedings. That written record (and all other evidence) is preserved at least long enough for all ___24___ to be exhausted, or for some further period of time provided by law (for example, in some U.S. states, death penalty statutes provide that all evidence must be ___25___ for an extended period of time). Most courts of record have rules of ___26___, and therefore they require that most parties be represented by counsel (specifically, attorneys holding a license to practice law before the specific tribunal). In contrast, in courts not of record, oral proceedings are not recorded, and the ___27___ makes his or her decision based on notes and memory. In most "not of record" proceedings, the ___28___ may appear personally, without lawyers. For example, most small claims courts, traffic courts, justice courts ___29___ over by justices of the peace, many administrative tribunals that make initial governmental administrative decisions such as government benefit determinations, and the like, are not ___30___ of record.(1)

21.	22.	23.	24.	25.
a. note	a. pre-served	a. aurel	a. contradictions	a. contracted
b. record	b. presserved	b. oral	b. appeals	b. appealed
c. summary	c. presarved	c. oraul	c. settlements	c. settled
d. memo	d. preserved	d. aural	d. objections	d. preserved

Passage 2

26.	27.	28.	29.	30.
a. preceeding	a. attorney	a. lawyers	a. precided	a. court
b. president	b. D.A.	b. parties	b. preceeded	b. courts
c. procedure	c. plaintiff	c. judges	c. presided	c. clerks
d. pressident	d. judge	d. precedents	d. pressided	d. courted

▲

Questions 31 - 35: Applying Facts and Information to Given Situations

"Directions: Use the information preceding each question to answer the question. Only that information should be used in answering the questions. Do not use any prior knowledge you may have on the subject. Choose the alternative that best answers the question."*

Question 31

Passport Application Procedure (Effective July 1, 2019)

You must apply in person using Form DS-11 if at least one of the following is true:

You are applying for your first U.S. passport

You are under age 16

Your previous U.S. passport was issued when you were under age 16

Your previous U.S. passport was lost, stolen, or damaged

Your previous U.S. passport was issued more than 15 years ago

If none of the above statements apply to you, you may be eligible to Renew using Form DS-82.

Please note: If you live in another country (including Canada) and you're submitting Form DS-11, you must apply in person at a U.S. embassy or consulate.(2)

Situation

On September 6, 2019, a Court Officer is assigned to security near the Passport Counter of the Bronx County Clerk Office. An elderly person in a wheelchair has a question regarding passports. Because the line at that counter is very long, she asks the Court Officer, "My passport is expired and was issued in April 6, 2001. Must I file for passport in person, or can I apply for the passport by mail?

31. Based on the preceding Passport Application Procedure and situation, what is the best course of action for the Court Officer to take?

A. The Court Officer should inform the person that because of her disability, she may request a waiver of the rules.

B. The Court Officer should inform the person that all passport applications must be filed by mail.

C. The Court Officer should inform that person that under the Passport Application Procedure (Effective July 1, 2019), he is prohibited from discussing passport requirements.

D. The Court Officer should draw the person's attention to Passport Application Procedure (Effective July 1, 2019).

Question 32

Small Claims cases filing fees:

The fee to start a case in City Court is:

- $15 for claims up to $1000, and
- $20 for claims between $1000 and $5000.

The fee to start a case in a Town or Village Court is:

- $10 for claims up to $1000, and
- $15 for claims between $1000 and $3000.

Situation

You are a Court Officer assigned to the entrance of a court building that houses the City Court, as well as the Village Court. A person entering the building asks, "I have a money order for $25.00 to start two cases in the Village Court. Is that the right amount?"

32. Based on the preceding procedure and situation, what would be a correct response?

A. Amount is correct if the person is starting two cases, each for claims between $1000 and $3000.

B. Amount is correct if the person is starting two cases, one for a claim for an amount up to $1,000 maximum and one for a claim between $1000 and $3000.

C. Amount is correct if the person is starting two cases, each for up to a maximum of $1,000.00.

D. none of the above

Questions 33 - 35

Case Records Filing Procedure

Civil case files for filing year 2019 shall be maintained as follows:

Case file numbers 1 - 4,000 shall be stored in room 1005. Case file numbers 4,001 - 8,000 shall be stored in room 1006, and case file numbers 8,001 and above shall be kept in room 1007.

The exceptions to this file storage requirement are files which contain subpoenaed records and files that have been designated as "Sensitive" or "Extra Security Required" files.
Files that contain subpoenaed records must be stored in Subpoenaed Records Room 1104.
"Sensitive" files must be stored in the Chief Clerk's Safe in room 1306, and "Extra Security Required" files must be stored in the Court Officer Safe in room 1307.

All files are public records and may be viewed by any member of the public. Exceptions are files that contain subpoenaed records, "Sensitive" files, and "Extra Security Required" files. These files may only be viewed by persons with a court order signed by the Judge presiding in the Part where the case is being tried or with a court order signed by the Judge assigned to the Special Term Part.

No files may be removed from the rooms where they are stored without an order from one of the above two Judges specifically stating the conditions and terms that must be followed to maintain continuous security of the files.

Situation

Attorney Vance Gibson represents the plaintiff in the Part where Court Officer Thomas Melnor is assigned. He shows Court Officer Melnor an order signed by Judge Frances Madison, the Judge presiding in the Part, permitting him to view and copy the file relating to the case. The file is in room 1307. Court Officer Melnor accompanies attorney Gibson so that security may be maintained over the file. After viewing the file, the attorney tries to copy the file using the copy machine in the room. However, the machine is not working and needs repair. He informs Court Officer Melnor that he must take the file to the sixth floor where there is another public copy machine.

33. Based on the preceding procedure and situation, what would be a correct response from Court Officer Melnor?

A. Allow the attorney to go to the sixth floor copy machine since he has a signed order from Judge Madison.

B. Allow the attorney to take the file to the sixth floor copy machine only if he, the Court Officer, accompanies him.

C. Allow him to go to the sixth floor with the file because attorneys are "Officers of the Court."

D. none of the above

Situation

File number 4,006 of 2019 has been designated a "Sensitive File."

34. Based on the above procedure, the file must be stored in room:

A. 1307

B. 1006

C. 1306

D. 1007

Situation

Attorney Vance Gibson shows Court Officer Melnor a signed court order, permitting him to view a file designated as an "Extra Security Required" file.

35. Based on the above Procedure and Situation, Court Officer must confirm that the order was signed by:

A. any Judge

B. the Supervising Judge

C. the Administrative Judge

D. None of the above are correct.

▲

For questions 36 - 40, read the passage and then answer the questions based solely on the information provided in the passage.

Passage for questions 36-37

A law enforcement officer or peace officer in North American English, is a public-sector employee whose duties primarily involve the enforcement of laws. The phrase can include police officers, municipal law enforcement officers and others. Security guards are civilians and therefore not law enforcement officers, unless they have been granted powers to enforce particular laws, such as those accredited under a community safety accreditation scheme such as a Security Police Officer. Modern legal codes use the term peace officer to include every person vested by the legislating state with law enforcement authority—traditionally, anyone who can arrest, or refer such arrest for a criminal prosecution. Hence, city police officers, county sheriffs' deputies, and state troopers are usually vested with the same authority within a given jurisdiction. Contract security officers may enforce certain laws and administrative regulations, which may include detainment or apprehension authority, including arresting. Peace officers may also be able to perform all duties that a law enforcement officer is tasked with, but may or may not be armed with a weapon. (1)

36. According to the above passage, which of the following statements is not correct?

A. The term "law enforcement officer or peace officer" can include police officers.

B. Contract security officers may enforce certain laws and administrative regulations,

C. Security guards are not law enforcement officers.

D. Peace officers must be armed with a weapon.

37. Which of the following titles would serve as the best title for the above passage?

A. Security Guards in North America

B. The duties of Police Officers

C. Peace Officers and Law Enforcement Officers

D. Contract Security Officers

Passage for questions 38-40

Although different legal processes aim to resolve many kinds of legal disputes, the legal procedures share some common features. All legal procedure, for example, is concerned with due process. Absent very special conditions, a court cannot impose a penalty - civil or criminal - against an individual who has not received notice of a lawsuit being brought against them, or who has not received a fair opportunity to present evidence for themselves. The standardization for the means by which cases are brought, parties are informed, evidence is presented, and facts are determined is intended to maximize the fairness of any proceeding.

Nevertheless, strict procedural rules have certain drawbacks. For example, they impose specific time limitations upon the parties that may either hasten or (more frequently) slow down the pace of proceedings. Furthermore, a party who is unfamiliar with procedural rules may run afoul of guidelines that have nothing to do with the merits of the case, and yet the failure to follow these guidelines may severely damage the party's chances.

Procedural systems are constantly torn between arguments that judges should have greater discretion in order to avoid the rigidity of the rules, and arguments that judges should have less discretion in order to avoid an outcome based more on the personal preferences of the judge than on the law or the facts.

Legal procedure, in a larger sense, is also designed to effect the best distribution of judicial resources. For example, in most courts of general jurisdiction in the United States, criminal cases are given priority over civil cases, because criminal defendants stand to lose their freedom, and should therefore be accorded the first opportunity to have their case heard. (1)

38. Which of the following statements is not supported by the above passage?

A. Failure to follow procedural guidelines may severely damage a party's chances in the case.

B. Some legal procedures in different jurisdictions share some common features.

C. Civil cases are given priority over criminal cases.

D. Strict procedural rules have drawbacks.

39. Which of the following titles would serve as the best title for the above passage?

A. Substantive Law

B. Civil, Family, and Criminal Law

C. Legal Procedural Rules

D. The Role of Substantive Law

40. According to the above passage, which of the following statements is correct?

A. Due process is not a concern of legal procedure.

B. Procedural rules may be strict or rigid.

C. Procedural rules always speed up proceedings.

D. All criminal cases involve felony offenses.

▲

Questions 41 - 60: Clerical Checking

Directions: The following example consists of five sets of information. Compare the information in the three sets, and on your answer sheet, mark:

Choice A: if none of the three sets are exactly alike

Choice B: if only the second and third sets are exactly alike

Choice C: if only the first and second sets are exactly alike

Choice D: if all the sets are exactly alike.

41. Attorney Wayne Fry Court Rules: 702.29 (917) 852-5943 Colton Village, NY	41. Attorney Wayne Fry Court Rules: 702.29 (917) 852-5943 Colton Village, NY	41. Attorney Wayne Fry Court Rules: 702.29 **(917) 852-5943** Coulton Village, NY
42. Barry S. Landmere Surrogates Court Court Interpreter Manitoba, NY 11363	42. *Barry S. Landmere* Surrogates Count Court Interpreter Manitoba, NY 11363	42. Barry S. Landnere Surrogates Court Court Interpreter Manitoba, NY 11363
43. 3289 Ospice Blvd. *Larry Cumberd, JHO* 5748291812228J. Traderof, Charles	43. 3289 Ospice Blvd. Larry Cumberd, JHO 5748291812228J. Traderoff, Charles	43. 3289 Ospice Blvd. Larry Cumberd, JHO 5748291812228J. Traderoff, Charles
44. Franklin and Merck Court of Claims, NY Hartsdale, NY 10530 (964) 382-1565	44. Franklin and Merck **Court of Claims, NY** Hartsdale, NY 10530 (964) 382-1565	44. Franklin and Merck Court of Claims, NY Hartsdale, NY 10530 (964) 382-1565
45. 893 East Hartford NY Hearing Examiner **CO Rudolph 25287A** Appellate Division	45. 893 East Hartford NY Hearing Examiner CO Rudolph 25287A Appellate Division	45. 893 East Hartford NY *Hearing Examiner* CO Rudolf 25287A Appellate Division

Directions: The following example consists of five sets of information. Compare the information in the three sets, and on your answer sheet, mark:

Choice A: if all the sets are exactly alike.

Choice B: if only the second and third sets are exactly alike

Choice C: if only the first and second sets are exactly alike

Choice D: if none of the three sets are exactly alike

46. J. Kevin L. McArthur **NYS Court Rules** Parking Permit D-2 Denser, William	46. J. Kevin I. McArthur NYS Court Rules Parking Permit D-2 Denser, William	46. J. Kevin L. McArther NYS Court Rules Parking Permit D-2 *Denser, William*
47. Middletown, 10940 2853 Sullivan Avenue Assault first degree (716) 289-3749	47. Middletown, 10940 2853 Sullivan Avenue Assault first degree (716) 289-3749	47. Middletown, 10940 2853 Sullivan Avenue Assault first degree (716) 289-3749
48. Queens Blvd., NY Files 28392-46853 5/3/2019, 7/12/19 *Principal Court Clerk*	48. Queens Blvd., NY **Files 28392-46853** 5/3/2019, 7/21/19 Principal Court Clerk	48. Queens Blvd., NY Files 28392-46853 5/3/2019, 7/21/19 Principal Court Clerk
49. Parts 27B, 22D, 37D Examiner S. Pollito Syracuse and Albany 756 Watertown Street	49. Parts 27B, 22D, 37D Examiner S. Pollito Syracuse and Albany 756 Watertown Street	49. Parts 27B, 22D, 37D Examiner S. Polito Syracuse and Albany 756 Watertown Street
50. (914) 389-2759 Arraignment Part 7C Ref. Numb. 358913 Archives Location 81	50. (914) 389-2759 Arraignment Part 7C *Ref. Numb. 358913* Archives Location 81	50. (914) 389-2795 **Arraignment Part 7C** Ref. Numb. 358913 Archives Location 81

Directions: The following example consists of five sets of information. Compare the information in the three sets, and on your answer sheet, mark:

Choice A: if only the first and second sets are exactly alike

Choice B: if only the second and third sets are exactly alike

Choice C: if all the sets are exactly alike.

Choice D: if none of the three sets are exactly alike

51. Magistrate Davidson *VTL Amend. 48-21* License C8KN89N Boris R. Kuznetsov	51. Magistrate Davidson VTL Amend. 48-21 License C8KN89N **Boris R. Kuznetsov**	51. Magistrate Davidson VTL Amend. 48-21 License C8KN89N Boris B. Kuznetsov
52. Part 19 (3/29/2020) 3492 S. Kingsbridge Section 4725-17637 Ivanov & Brand, PC	52. Part 19 (3/29/2020) 3492 S. Kingsbridge Section 4725-17637 Ivanov & Brand, PC	52. Part 19 (3/29/2020) *3492 S. Kingsbridge* Section 4725-17637 Ivanov & Brand, PC
53. (646) (914) & (934) Poor Person Petition **4869 Winston Circle** Captain Sinonstein	53. (646) (914) & (934) Poor Person Petition 4869 Winston Circle Captain Simonstein	53. (646) (914) & (934) Poor Person Petition 4869 Winston Circle Captain Simonstein
54. Parts 34A, 19D, 27C Sergeant Frank Elder 2756-4 Battavia Ave. (838) 649-5835 Ext. 6	54. Parts 34A, 19D, 27C *Sergeant Frank Elder* 2756-4 Batavia Ave. (838) 649-5835 Ext. 6	54. Parts 34A, 19D, 27C Sergeant Frank Elder 2756-4 Batavia Ave. (838) 649-5835 Ext. 6
55. Nassau Section 334 Ms. Tamanta Norfolk Ref. Numb. 3534173 FCA FO-13794/20	55. Nassau Section 334 Ms. Tamanta Norfolk Ref. Numb. 3534713 FCA FO-13794/20	55. **Nassau Section 334** Ms. Tamanta Norfolk Ref. Numb. 3534713 FCA FD-13794/20

Directions: The following example consists of five sets of information. Compare the information in the three sets, and on your answer sheet, mark:

Choice A: if only the second and third sets are exactly alike

Choice B: if only the first and second sets are exactly alike

Choice C: if all the sets are exactly alike.

Choice D: if none of the three sets are exactly alike

56. Attempted Bribery PL Section 50.05(b) *George S. Nukofsky* 763976258967-L	56. **Attempted Bribery** PL Section 50.05(b) George S. Nukosfky 763976258967-L	56. Attempted Bribery PL Section 50.02(b) George S. Nukofsky 763976258967-L
57. Santoffsky, Gregory 8629 Bedoni Drive Criminal Possession Landlord and Tenant	57. Santoffsky, Gregory 8629 Bedoni Drive Criminal Possession Landlord and Tenant	57. Santoffsky, Gregory 8629 Bedoni Drive Criminal Possession Landlord and Tenant
58. 140 Grand St. 10601 Files 28497-28502 **8/12/19, 8/21/19** CA Harriet Beeker	58. 140 Grand St. 10601 *Files 28497-28502* 8/12/19, 8/21/19 CA Harriet Beeker	58. 140 Grand St. 10601 Files 28497-28502 8/12/19, 8/21/19 CA Harriet Beaker
59. 3827 West 15th Ave. Doctor B. Sussman 7859038175982-GSA	59. 3827 West 15th Ave. Doctor B. Sussman 785903875982-GSA	59. 3827 West 15th Ave. *Doctor B. Sussman* 785903875982-GSA
60. Wednesday Calendar ARB. 430578-496 Elmont, Queens NY Capital of New York	60. Wednesday Calendar ARB. 430578-496 Elmont, Queens NY Capital of New York	60. Wednesday Calendar ARB. 430578-496 **Elmont, Queens NY** Capitol of New York

Questions 61-75: Record Keeping

The following pages contain the following:

1. Three individual tables listing cases that appeared before Trial Judges

   in Criminal, Family, Civil Courts (October 21, 2019 - October 25, 2019).

2. A coding table "Coding Table: Part / Judge Presiding".

3. Two summary tables to organize the information presented in the first three tables listing cases that

   appeared before Judges in Criminal, Family, Civil Courts (October 21, 2019 - October 25, 2019)).

Directions: Complete the two summary tables based on the information provided and then answer the ten questions that follow.

Note that only the answers to the ten questions will be graded and not the work done on the tables.

Criminal Court List of Cases On the Court Calendar October 21, 2019 - October 25, 2019			
Judge Presiding	**Date Case Filed**	**Case Disposition**	**Fine Imposed**
Zelinski	9/8/17	Adjourned	
Garcia	2/26/17	Trial	$ 1,500
Zelinski	9/5/17	Adjourned	
Garcia	5/13/18	Dismissed	
Zelinski	5/8/19	Trial	$ 2,400
Garcia	1/16/18	Trial	$ 3,000
Garcia	1/27/18	Dismissed	
Zelinski	4/27/18	Trial	
Zelinski	6/20/19	Dismissed	
Garcia	6/22/19	Adjourned	
Zelinski	9/22/19	Trial	$ 2,500
Garcia	11/19/19	Adjourned	

Family Court List of Cases On the Court Calendar October 21, 2019 - October 25, 2019			
Judge Presiding	**Date Case Filed**	**Case Disposition**	**Amount of Restitution Ordered**
Liang	12/4/18	Trial	$ 1,250
Russo	12/9/18	Trial	
Russo	12/22/18	Adjourned	
Liang	1/25/19	Trial	$ 1,500
Russo	1/29/19	Dismissed	
Russo	2/5/19	Adjourned	
Russo	6/22/19	Adjourned	
Liang	7/14/19	Trial	$ 1,250
Liang	8/25/19	Dismissed	
Russo	8/29/19	Trial	$ 1,000
Russo	9/2/19	Dismissed	
Liang	9/6/19	Adjourned	
Russo	10/1/19	Trial	$ 3,000

	Civil Court List of Cases On the Court Calendar October 21, 2019 - October 25, 2019		
Judge Presiding	**Date Case Filed**	**Case Disposition**	**Settlement Award Amount**
Jefferson	3/24/17	Settled	
Fulton	4/19/17	Adjourned	
Fulton	3/16/18	Dismissed	
Jefferson	4/21/18	Dismissed	
Fulton	7/3/18	Settled	$ 12,500
Jefferson	2/21/19	Adjourned	
Fulton	3/17/19	Settled	$ 9,200
Jefferson	4/13/19	Adjourned	
Fulton	6/12/19	Settled	$ 9,900
Jefferson	6/15/19	Defaulted	
Jefferson	6/18/19	Settled	
Fulton	8/2/2019	Settled	$ 7,100

Coding Table Part / Judge Presiding	
Part	**Judge Presiding**
C4	Fulton
C7	Jefferson
F1	Russo
F2	Liang
R4	Zelinski
R6	Garcia

Summary Table 1:

Cases on Calendar October 21, 2019 - October 25, 2019				
Case Status	**Criminal**	**Family**	**Civil**	**Total Cases**
Adjourned				
Defaulted				
Dismissed				
Settled - with Money Award				
Settled - no money award				
Trial with Fine Imposed				
Trial with no fine imposed				
Trial with Restitution Ordered				
Trial with no Restitution Ordered				
Total Cases				
Cases by Date Filed				
2017				
2018				
2019				
Total Cases				

Summary Table 2:

Part Code	Cases On Calendar October 21, 2019 - October 25, 2019					
	Adjourned	Defaulted	Dismissed	Settled Money Award	Trial with Fine Imposed	Trial with Restitution Ordered
C4						
C7						
F1						
F2						
R4						
R6						

(Note that in the above table only certain case status' are included.)

Questions 61 - 75

61. What is the total number of cases "Trial with Restitution Ordered"?

    A. 3   C. 5

    B. 4   D. 6

62. What is the total number of cases filed in all courts in 2017 and 2019?

    A. 15   C. 25

    B. 32   D. 27

63. Which Judge had four cases "Settled with money award"?
    A. Jefferson   C. Liang
    B. Fulton   D. Garcia

64. Which Judge has a part with code F2?
    A. Jefferson   C. Liang
    B. Zelinski   D. Russo

65. What is the total number of cases "Settled- with money award" and "Settled - no money award"?
    A. 6   C. 7
    B. 5   D. none of the above

66. The total of criminal court cases plus civil court cases exceeds the number of family court cases
    by_____.
    A. 12   C. 10
    B. 11   D. 9

67. What is the total number of civil cases that were "Adjourned" or "Defaulted"?
    A. 3   C. 5
    B. 4   D. 6

68. What is the total number of cases in all three courts that were filed in 2019?
    A. 20   C. 24
    B. 21   D. 22

69. How many cases were "Dismissed" in Family Court?
    A. 1   C. 3
    B. 2   D. 4

70. The number of cases "Trial with Fine Imposed" exceeds the number of cases "Trial with no fine
    imposed" by _____.
    A. 2   C. 4
    B. 3   D. 1

71. Part Code C4 had how many cases "Settled money award"?

   A. 3   C. 2

   B. 4   D. none of the above

72. Which court had the greatest number of cases filed in one year?

   A. Family Court   C. Court of Claims

   B. Civil Court   D. Criminal Court

73. What is the total number of cases for all three courts?.

   A. 38   C. 36

   B. 35   D. 37

74. What is the Part Code for the part that had "Settled money award" cases?

   A. C7   C. R4

   B. F1   D. C4

75. What is the total number of cases "Dismissed" for all three courts?

   A. 4   C. 6

   B. 8   D. 7

END OF QUESTIONS FOR PRACTICE TEST 3

ANSWERS: PRACTICE TEST 3

1. D. Queens County	6. B. Part 16	11. D. Martinez
2. B. two hundred fifty	7. D. fourth floor	12. A. Sergeant Foster
3. B. Warriors for Justice	8. C. November 5, 2019	13. B. email
4. A. T-shirt	9. A. Eleanor Grant	14. A. 9:30 a.m.
5. C. wrists	10. D. Arnold Powell	15. C. Beltway Street

16. b. is (singular, present tense, and logic of sentence)

17. d. jurisdiction (correct spelling and meaning)

18. b. democratic (vocabulary, correct meaning)

19. d. acuity (correct spelling)

20. b. university (logic of sentence)

21. b. record (logic: official record, as also referred to in the next sentence)

22. d. preserved (correct spelling and vocabulary)

23. b. oral (vocabulary and spelling)

24. b. appeals (vocabulary and subject of passage)

25. d. preserved (logic of sentence)

26. c. procedure (logic, vocabulary)

27. d. judge (logic)

28. b. parties (logic of sentence)

29. c. presided (vocabulary)

30. b. courts (logic, continuity, grammar)

31. D. The Court Officer should draw the person's attention to Passport Application Procedure (Effective July 1, 2019).

    Choice "A" is not correct because the procedure does not mention waiver of the rules.

    Choice "B" is incorrect according to the procedure.

    Choice "C" is not mentioned in the procedure.

32. B. Amount is correct if the person is starting two cases, one for a claim for an amount up to $1,000 maximum and one for a claim between $1000 and $3000. ($10 + $15 = $25)

33. D. none of the above

    Choices "A," "B", and "C" are not correct because the procedure states, "No files may be removed from the rooms where they are stored without an order from one of the above two Judges specifically stating the conditions and terms that must be followed to maintain continuous security of the files."

34. C. 1306

    "Sensitive" files must be stored in the Chief Clerk's Safe in room 1306."

35. D. None of the above are correct.

    "All files are public records and may be viewed by any member of the public. Exceptions are files that contain subpoenaed records, "Sensitive" files, and "Extra Security Required" files. These files may only be viewed by persons with a court order signed by the Judge presiding in the Part where the case is being tried or with a court order signed by the Judge assigned to the Special Term Part.

36. D. Peace officers must be armed with a weapon.

    This is not correct because the passage states, "Peace officers may also be able to perform all duties that a law enforcement officer is tasked with, but may or may not be armed with a weapon."

37. C. Peace Officers and Law Enforcement Officers

Choices "A," "B", and "D" are not correct because they refer to only a part of the passage.

38. C. Civil cases are given priority over criminal cases.

This statement is not supported because the passage states the opposite, "Criminal cases are given priority over civil cases."

39. C. Legal Procedural Rules

Choices "A," is not a good title because the passage deals with Procedures and not Substantive Law. "B" is not a good title because, among other reasons, Family Law is not mentioned. "D" is not a good choice because the passage deals with procedural laws and rules.

40. B. Procedural rules may be strict or rigid.

The passage states, "...strict procedural rules have certain drawbacks."

41. Choice C: if only the first and second sets are exactly alike

Colton Village, NY   Colton Village, NY   C**ou**lton Village, NY

42. Choice A: if none of the three sets are exactly alike

Barry S. Landmere   Barry S. Landmere   Barry S. Land**dne**re

Surrogates Court   Surrogates Co**unt**   Surrogates Court

43. Choice B: if only the second and third sets are exactly alike

Trade**rof,** Charles   Traderoff, Charles   Traderoff, Charles

44. Choice D: if all the sets are exactly alike.

45. Choice C: if only the first and second sets are exactly alike

CO Rudolph 25287A CO Rudolph 25287A   CO Rud**olf** 25287A

46. Choice D: if none of the three sets are exactly alike

J. Kevin L. McArthur   J. Kevin **I.** McArthur   J. Kevin L. McArt**her**

47. Choice A: if all the sets are exactly alike.

48. Choice B: if only the second and third sets are exactly alike

5/3/2019, 7/**12**/19   5/3/2019, 7/21/19   5/3/2019, 7/21/19

49. Choice C: if only the first and second sets are exactly alike

Examiner S. Pollito   Examiner S. Pollito   Examiner S. Po**lito**

50. Choice C: if only the first and second sets are exactly alike

(914) 389-2759   (914) 389-2759   (914) 389-27**95**

51. Choice A: if only the first and second sets are exactly alike

Boris R. Kuznetsov   Boris R. Kuznetsov   Boris **B.** Kuznetsov

52. Choice C: if all the sets are exactly alike.

53. Choice B: if only the second and third sets are exactly alike

Captain S**ino**nstein   Captain Simonstein   Captain Simonstein

54. Choice B: if only the second and third sets are exactly alike

    2756-4 Ba**tta**via Ave.   2756-4 Batavia Ave.   2756-4 Batavia Ave.

55. Choice D: if none of the three sets are exactly alike

    Ref. Numb. 3534**173**   Ref. Numb. 3534713   Ref. Numb. 3534713

    FCA FO-13794/20   FCA FO-13794/20   FCA **FD**-13794/20

56. Choice D: if none of the three sets are exactly alike

    PL Section 50.05(b)   PL Section 50.05(b)   PL Section 50.**02**(b)

    George S. Nukofsky   George S. Nuk**osf**ky   George S. Nukofsky

57. Choice C: if all the sets are exactly alike.

58. Choice B: if only the first and second sets are exactly alike

    CA Harriet Beeker   CA Harriet Beeker   CA Harriet B**ea**ker

59. Choice A: if only the second and third sets are exactly alike

    785903**817**5982-GSA 785903875982-GSA 785903875982-GSA

60. Choice B: if only the first and second sets are exactly alike

    Capital of New York   Capital of New York   Capi**to**l of New York

Completed Summary Tables

Summary Table 1:

Cases on Calendar October 21, 2019 - October 25, 2019				
Case Status	**Criminal**	**Family**	**Civil**	**Total Cases**
Adjourned	|||| 4	|||| 4	||| 3	11
Defaulted			| 1	1
Dismissed	||| 3	||| 3	|| 2	8
Settled - with money award			|||| 4	4
Settled - no money award			|| 2	2
Trial with Fine Imposed	|||| 4			4
Trial with no fine imposed	| 1			1
Trial with restitution ordered		||||| 5		5
Trial with no restitution ordered		| 1		1
Total Cases	12	13	12	37
Cases by Date Filed				
2017	||| 3		|| 2	5
2018	|||| 4	||| 3	||| 3	10
2019	||||| 5	||||| ||||| 10	||||| || 7	22
Total Cases	12	13	12	37

Summary Table 2:

Part Code	Adjourned	Defaulted	Dismissed	Settled money award	Trial with fine imposed	Trial with restitution ordered
C4 Fulton	| 1		| 1	|||| 4		
C7 Jefferson	|| 2	| 1	| 1			
F1 Russo	||| 3		|| 2			|| 2
F2 Liang	| 1		| 1			||| 3
R4 Zelinski	|| 2		| 1		|| 2	
R6 Garcia	|| 2		|| 2		|| 2	

61. C. 5	69. C. 3
62. D. 27 (5 + 22 = 27)	70. B. 3 (4 - 1 = 3)
63. B. Fulton	71. B. 4
64. C. Liang	72. A. Family Court (10 cases)
65. A. 6 (4 = 2)	73. D. 37 (12 + 13 + 12 = 37)
66. B. 11 (12 + 12 = 24, less 13 = 11)	74. D. C4 (Judge Fulton)
67. B. 4 (3 + 1 = 4)	75. B. 8
68. D. 22 (5 + 10 + 7 = 22)	

END OF ANSWERS FOR PRACTICE TEST 3

PRACTICE TEST 4: QUESTIONS
(75 Questions: Time allowed: 3.5 hours)

Questions 1-15: Remembering Facts and Information

"Directions: Read the brief story below. Study it for five minutes. Then, turn the story over and wait for ten minutes before you answer the fifteen questions on the following page. Try to remember as many details of the incident without making any written notes."*

(**Written test**: At the end of the five minutes, the test monitor will collect this sheet and ten minutes after that, you will be instructed to begin the test by answering from memory the first fifteen questions relating to this story.

Computer test: At the end of the five minutes, the passage will disappear from the screen and ten minutes after that, you will be instructed to begin the test by answering from memory the first fifteen questions relating to this story.)

Tuesday, December 3, 2019, proved to be a very busy day at the Family Court building at 379 West End Avenue in the Bronx, New York. The day before, on Monday afternoon, a small fire in the basement of the Criminal Court building across the street from the Family Court building damaged the main electrical panel. The Criminal Court building was fully evacuated and the fire was put out in less than an hour. However, upon inspection of the fire damage, the Fire Department Chief determined that the panel was damaged beyond repair and had to be replaced - something that would take at least two days.

Because the criminal building would not be useable until the panel was replaced, the Deputy Administrative Judge adjourned the Thursday and Friday calendars for some criminal court parts and temporarily relocated seven other parts to the Family Court building. The criminal parts that were relocated were those where the defendants were not incarcerated and therefore no holding pens or extra officers were required. Two of these parts were the DAT Part and the Summons Part.

Captain Harry Reynolds from the Family Court was assigned to facilitate the operation of the criminal parts. He worked in tandem with Captain Ellen Spivek of criminal court who had worked in the Family Court building for three years before being voluntarily reassigned to the criminal court.

On Thursday, at 2:00 p.m., the Administrative Judge visited both buildings. He noted that the repairs to the electrical panel were proceeding timely and that the relocated parts were operating smoothly. At the Family Court Chief Clerk's Office, he thanked everyone from both courts for working hard to ensure the continuing operation of the criminal court. He remarked that without the professionally trained and capable Court Officers, much of this success would not have been possible.

Answer questions 1-15 based on the information provided in the passage which you have read.

1. What is the name of the female Captain in criminal court??

A. Helen Speck   C. Ellen Spivek

B. Eleanor Spock   D. none of the above

2. On what day did the fire occur?

A. November 3, 2019   C. November 2, 2019

B. December 3, 2019   D. December 2, 2019

3. The Family Court building is located on which avenue?

A. West Avenue   C. Best Way Avenue

B. West End Avenue   D. none of the above

4. The fire in the criminal court building was put out in less than _____.

A. two hours   C. one hour

B. three hours   D. none of the above

5. The calendars for two days were adjourned. These two days were:

A. Tuesday and Wednesday   C. Monday and Tuesday

B. Wednesday and Thursday   D. Thursday and Friday

6. The criminal parts that were relocated were the DAT and the _____.

A. Desk Appearance Part   C. Misdemeanor Part

B. Summons Part   D. none of the above

7. On what day did the Administrative Judge visit both buildings?

A. Wednesday   C. Friday

B. Thursday   D. none of the above

8. At what time did the Administrative Judge visit both buildings?

A. 2:00 p.m.   C. 1:00 p.m.

B. 3:00 p.m.   D. none of the above

9. Captain Harry Reynolds was from which court?

A. Civil Court   C. Family Court

B. Criminal Court   D. none of the above

10. What did the fire damage?

A. main electrical switch

B. main electrical panel

C. main secondary panel

D. none of the above

11. The replacement of the panel would take at least _____.

A. one day

B. two days

C. three days

D. none of the above

12. How many parts were temporarily relocated to the Family Court building?

A. five

B. six

C. seven

D. none of the above

13. The female Captain worked in the Family Court building for how many years before being reassigned to the criminal court?

A. one

B. two

C. three

D. none of the above

14. At the Family Court _____ Office, the Administrative Judge thanked everyone from both courts.

A. Chief Clerk's

B. Captain's

C. Major's

D. none of the above

15. The small fire occurred _____.

A. on the first floor

B. on the second floor

C. in the basement

D. none of the above

Questions 16 - 30: Reading, Understanding and Interpreting Written Material

"Directions: The three passages below each contain five numbered blanks. Below each passage are listed five sets of words numbered to match the blanks. Pick the word from each set which seems to make the most sense both in the sentence and the total paragraph."*

Passage 1

Public service is a service intended to serve all members of ___16___ community. It is usually provided by government to people living within its ___17___, either directly (through the public sector) or by financing provision of services. The term is ___18___ with a social consensus (usually expressed through democratic elections) that certain ___19___ should be available to all, regardless of ___20___, physical ability or mental acuity.

16.	17.	18.	19.	20.
a. all	a. juristiction	a. differentiated	a. service	a. priority
b. two	b. jurisdiction	b. separate	b. services	b. order
c. several	c. juresticson	c. associated	c. plan	c. listing
d. a	d. jurisidiction	d. severed	d. right	d. income

Passage 2

A jury is a sworn ___21___ of people convened to render an impartial verdict (a finding of fact on a question) officially submitted to them by a court, or to set a penalty or judgment. Most trial ___22___ are "petit juries", and usually consist of twelve people. A larger jury known as a grand jury was used to investigate potential crimes and render indictments against suspects, but all common law countries except the United States and Liberia have phased these out. The modern ___23___ court jury arrangement ___24___ evolved out of the medieval juries in England. Members were supposed to inform themselves of ___25___ and then of the details of the crimes. Their function was therefore closer to that of a grand jury than that of a jury in a trial.

21.	22.	23.	24.	25.
a. list	a. plaintiffs	a. civil	a. hasn't	a. plaintiffs
b. index	b. juries	b. family	b. had	b. crimes
c. crowd	c. defendants	c. criminal	c. hadn't	c. claimants
d. body	d. witnesses	d. small claims	d. has	d. judges

Passage 3

Throughout American history, it has been a tradition to pledge ____26____ to the American flag. Recently, some people are refusing to participate in the pledge for a variety of reasons, including political or ____27____ grounds. Many of them do not ____28____ the contribution that the American system has made to their well-being. These people include some very ____29____ billionaires. We should keep in mind that the flag is a symbol of our freedom and remain ____30____ to showing our appreciation at every opportunity that we get.

26.	27.	28.	29.	30.
a. allegaince	a. religous	a. acknowlege	a. successfull	a. commited
b. allegience	b. religius	b. acknowledge	b. succesful	b. committed
c. alegiance	c. religious	c. aknowledge	c. sucessful	c. comitted
d. allegiance	d. relligius	d. acknoledge	d. successful	d. comited

Questions 31 - 35: Applying Facts and Information to Given Situations

"Directions: Use the information preceding each question to answer the question. Only that information should be used in answering the questions. Do not use any prior knowledge you may have on the subject. Choose the alternative that best answers the question."*

Questions 31

Summary of Law: Who May File a Petition for Child Support?

When parents live separately and one parent has custody of the child, that parent, called the "custodial parent", may file a petition in Family Court asking the court to enter an order for the "non-custodial parent" to pay child support.

A child who is not emancipated and is living away from both parents may file a petition against his or her parents asking for an order of support to be paid to the child.

When a child is receiving public assistance benefits, or is living in a foster home and receiving foster care benefits, the Department of Social Services may file a petition against the non-custodial parent or parents asking that the court enter an order for child support to be paid to the government agency while it continues to pay benefits for the child.

The party filing the petition is called the "petitioner" and the party from whom support is sought is the "respondent". The petition must be served upon (delivered to) the respondent, together with a summons indicating the date of the court hearing."(3)

Situation 1

At the Family Court Information Counter, a young girl who qualifies by age as a "child" approaches Court Officer Georgina Barrows and asks her if she is permitted to file a petition for child support. She explains to Court Officer Barrows that she had to move out of her parents' house and is now living with her grandmother because of her parents' erratic behavior due to illegal drug use.

31. Based on the preceding summary of law and the situation, besides referring the person to the petition information counter, which of the following is the best response that Court Officer Barrows should give?

A. Because the child is living away from the parents, she should file a case in civil court and not family court.

B. She cannot file a case because she is a "child" and must be represented by an attorney.

C. She should file a claim in civil court for damages due to mental hardship.

D. She is authorized to file a family court petition for child support because she is an unemancipated child.

Situation 2

Another young person who qualifies as a "child" due to age, informs Court Officer Barrows that he is married and has been living with his wife for a year. He has fallen on hard financial times and now seeks to file a petition to compel his parents to provide support because of his age. He asks Court Officer Barrows if this is correct.

32. Besides referring the person to the petition information counter, which of the following is the best response that Court Officer Barrows should give?

A. The person can start a case because he is still a "child."

B. Both the wife and the "child" should initiate the case.

C. Refer the person to the Summary of Law: "Who May File a Petition for Child Support? and then refer him to the clerk at the petition counter.

D. none of the above

Questions 33

Civil Procedure (CPLR: Rule 2101. Form of papers)

(a) Quality, size and legibility. Each paper served or filed shall be durable, white and, except for summonses, subpoenas, notices of appearance, notes of issue, orders of protection, temporary orders of protection and exhibits, shall be eleven by eight and one-half inches in size. The writing shall be legible and in black ink. Beneath each signature shall be printed the name signed. The letters in the summons shall be in clear type of no less than twelve-point in size. Each other printed or typed paper served or filed, except an exhibit, shall be in clear type of no less than ten-point in size.

(b) Language. Each paper served or filed shall be in the English language which, where practicable, shall be of ordinary usage. Where an affidavit or exhibit annexed to a paper served or filed is in a foreign language, it shall be accompanied by an English translation and an affidavit by the translator stating his qualifications and that the translation is accurate.

Situation 1

A person who is not represented by an attorney, wishes to file a paper that he has served on the opposing party in his case. The paper is in Spanish, with an English translation attached. He asks a Court Officer if this is correct, according to rule 2101.

33. Based on the preceding procedure, which of the following is the best response by the Court Officer?
A. The paper is proper, according to CPLR 2101.
B. The paper is proper if it has attached to it an affidavit by the translator.
C. The paper is not proper according to CPLR 2101 because it must be in the English language.
D. none of the above

Situation 2

The same person, who is an artist and filing a claim for unpaid services, has a poster that she wishes to use as an exhibit. The poster is fourteen inches by fourteen inches. She asks if this meets the form requirements set forth in CPLR 2101.

34. Based on CPLR 2101 and the preceding situation, which of the following choices is correct?
A. The exhibit cannot be filed because it is larger than the prescribed size.
B. The exhibit can be used as evidence, but cannot be filed.
C. The exhibit can be filed because it meets the size requirements.
D. none of the above

35. Which of the following is not listed as an exception to the eleven by eight and one-half inches in size requirement?
A. orders of protection
B. subpoenas
C. summonses
D. complaints

For questions 36 - 40, read the passage and then answer the questions based solely on the information provided in the passage.

Passage for questions 36-37

A court is any person or institution with authority to judge or adjudicate, often as a government institution, with the authority to adjudicate legal disputes between parties and carry out the administration of justice in civil, criminal, and administrative matters in accordance with the rule of law. In both common law and civil law legal systems, courts are the central means for dispute resolution, and it is generally understood that all people have an ability to bring their claims before a court. Similarly, the rights of those accused of a crime include the right to present a defense before a court. The system of courts that interprets and applies the law is collectively known as the judiciary. The place where a court sits is known as a venue. The room where court proceedings occur is known as a courtroom, and the building as a courthouse; court facilities range from simple and very small facilities in rural communities to large buildings in cities.(1)

36. Based on the preceding passage, which of the following statements is not correct?
A. Court facilities range in size.
B. The judiciary is the system of courts.
C. A court is a person or an institution with authority to adjudicate.
D. Venue is the time at which a court session is held.

37. Based on the preceding passage, which of the following statements is not correct?
A. A court may be a government institution.
B. A court may adjudicate legal disputes between parties.
C. A person accused of a crime must be present before the court.
D. All of the above are correct.

Passage for questions 38-40

The two major legal traditions of the western world are the civil law courts and the common law courts. These two great legal traditions are similar, in that they are products of western culture although there are significant differences between the two traditions.

Civil law courts are profoundly based upon Roman Law, specifically a civil body of law entitled "Corpus iuris civilis". This theory of civil law was rediscovered around the end of the eleventh century and became a foundation for university legal education starting in Bologna, Spain and subsequently being taught throughout continental European Universities. Civil law is firmly ensconced in the French and German legal systems.

Common law courts were established by English royal judges of the King's Council after the Norman Invasion of Britain in 1066. The royal judges created a body of law by combining local customs they were made aware of through traveling and visiting local jurisdictions. This common standard of law became known as "Common Law". This legal tradition is practiced in the English and American legal systems.

In most civil law jurisdictions, courts function under an inquisitorial system. In the common law system, most courts follow the adversarial system. Procedural law governs the rules by which courts operate; civil procedure for private disputes (for example); and criminal procedure for violation of the criminal law. In recent years international courts are being created to resolve matters not covered by the jurisdiction of national courts. For example, The International Criminal Court, based in The Hague, in The Kingdom of The Netherlands.(1)

38. Which of the following titles is the best title for the preceding passage?

A. The Common Law Tradition

B. French and English Law

C. The Traditions of Law in the Western World

D. The Advantages of Civil Law

39. Based on the preceding passage, which of the following statements is not correct?

A. The law upon which courts operate is procedural law.

B. International courts resolve matters not covered within the jurisdiction of national courts.

C. The inquisitorial system is used in most civil jurisdictions.

D. Common law is based upon Roman Law.

40. According to the preceding passage:

A. The International Criminal Court, is based in The Prague.

B. Civil law and common law are the same.

C. Substantive law governs the rules by which courts operate.

D. Civil law and common law are usually used in different jurisdictions.

▲

Questions 41 - 60: Clerical Checking

Directions: The following example consists of five sets of information. Compare the information in the three sets, and on your answer sheet, mark:

Choice A: if none of the three sets are exactly alike

Choice B: if only the second and third sets are exactly alike

Choice C: if only the first and second sets are exactly alike

Choice D: if all the sets are exactly alike.

41. CPL and PL 2019 7825 Third Avenue Records 2019: B273 **Suffolk Village Court**	41. CPL and PL 2019 *7825 Third Avenue* Records 2019: B273 Suffolk Village Court	41. CPL and PL 2019 7825 Third Avenue Records 2019: B273 Suffolk Village Court
42. TSF: 6/12/19 - H-J 2871 Westminster St. Ct. Rep. Abrantes Cayuga & Chemong	42. TSF: 6/12/19 - H-J 2871 Westminster St. Ct. Rep. Abrantis Cayuga & Chemong	42. TSF: 6/12/19 - H-J 2871 Eastminster St. Ct. Rep. Abrantes Cayuga & Chemong
43. EPTL 225 N. 279.18 Martin S. Coltun LSA 4756/2221 9/16 B. Clinton, Referee	43. EPTL 225 N. 279.18 Martin S. Colton **LSA 4756/2221 9/16** B. Clinton, Referee	43. EPTL 225 N. 279.18 Martin S. Colton LSA 4756/2221 9/16 *B. Clinton, Referee*
44. Donner & Baxton 37421253832-4439 (976) 363-274-7128 CPLR 2429 & 2431	44. Donner & Baxton 37421253832-4439 (976) 363-274-7128 CPLR 2429 & 2431	44. Donner & Baxton 37421253832-4436 (976) 363-274-7128 CPLR 2429 & 2431
45. Helen Kospi, JHO Hearing Examiner *8756 Southview Ave.* (856) 386-9375 Ext. 2	45. Helen Kospi, JHO Hearing Examiner 8756 Southview Ave. (856) 386-9375 Ext. 2	45. Helen Kospi, JHO **Hearing Examiner** 8756 Southview Ave. (856) 386-9375 Ext. 5

Directions: The following example consists of five sets of information. Compare the information in the three sets, and on your answer sheet, mark:

Choice A: if all the sets are exactly alike.

Choice B: if only the second and third sets are exactly alike

Choice C: if only the first and second sets are exactly alike

Choice D: if none of the three sets are exactly alike

46. Judge Ted Masterson CR 205.87 (Limits) (386) 693-8269 X72 **Thompson, Marla**	46. Judge Ted Masterson *CR 205.87 (Limits)* (386) 693-8269 X72 Thompson, Marla	46. Judge Ted Masterson CR 205.87 (Limits) (386) 693-8269 X72 Thompson, Marla
47. 973689036552-38 1641 Kings Avenue Civil Rules 743-339 Feinstein, Margaret	47. 973689036552-38 1641 King Avenue Civil Rules 743-339 Feinstein, Margaret	47. 97368903652-38 1641 Kings Avenue Civil Rules 743-339 Feinstein, Margaret
48. Jamieson, Loretta Files 45593-48593 6/10/2019, 7/27/19 CR Irma Masters	48. Jamieson, Loretta Files 45593-448593 **6/10/2019, 7/27/19** CR Irma Masters	48. Jamieson, Loretta Files 45593-448593 6/10/2019, 7/27/19 CR Irma Masters
49. Parts 29N, 23B, 39A Examiner Moretto Westchester75082 849297753978	49. Parts 29N, 23B, 39A Examiner Moretto Westchester75082 849297753978	49. Parts 29N, 23B, 39A **Examiner Moretto** Westchester75082 849297753798
50. NYS Sect. 376-980 *Fernando Devine* Ref. Numb. 5493256 Criminal File A-62/19	50. NYS Sect. 376-980 Fernando Devine Ref. Numb. 5493256 Criminal File A-62/19	50. *NYS Sect. 376-980* Fernande Devine Ref. Numb. 5493256 Criminal File A-62/19

Directions: The following example consists of five sets of information. Compare the information in the three sets, and on your answer sheet, mark:

Choice A: if only the first and second sets are exactly alike

Choice B: if only the second and third sets are exactly alike

Choice C: if all the sets are exactly alike.

Choice D: if none of the three sets are exactly alike

51. Referee Hartman Rules Amend. 39-24 Plate D7KL89D Lora S. Martinoff	51. Referee Hartman **Rules Amend. 39-24** Plate D7KL89D Lora S. Martinof	51. Referee Hartmen Rules Amend. 39-24 Plate D7KL89D Lora S. Martinoff
52. Room 27 (4/16/2020) *2441 N. Queensland* Statute 2757-12669 Lorner & Vector, PC	52. Room 27 (4/16/2020) 2441 N. Queensland Statute 2757-12669 Lorner & Vector, PC	52. Room 27 (4/16/2020) 2441 N. Queensland Statutes 2757-12669 Lorner & Vector, PC
53. 2097 Godisky Ave. Files 68892-837142 9/15/2019, 11/24/19 CO Franklin Faustore	53. 2097 Godisky Ave. Files 68892-837142 9/15/2019, 11/24/19 *CO Franklin Faustore*	53. 2097 Godisky Ave. Files 68892-837142 9/15/2019, 11/24/19 CO Franklin Faustore
54. 978367429749 - 287 OCL Juanita Davila **Columbia, Chemung** 364-572-3328 Ext. 7	54. 978367429749 - 287 OCI Juanita Davila Columbia, Chemung 364-572-3328 Ext. 7	54. 978367429749 - 287 OCI Juanita Davila Columbia, Chemung **364-572-3328 Ext. 7**
55. Clinton Section 6409 Carla D. Benevento Ref. Numb. 354663 Crim. File F-23753/20	55. Clinton Section 6409 *Carla D. Benevento* Ref. Numb. 354663 Crim. File F-23753/20	55. Clinton Section 6409 Carla D. Benivento Ref. Numb. 354663 Crim. File F-23753/20

Directions: The following example consists of five sets of information. Compare the information in the three sets, and on your answer sheet, mark:

Choice A: if only the second and third sets are exactly alike

Choice B: if only the first and second sets are exactly alike

Choice C: if all the sets are exactly alike.

Choice D: if none of the three sets are exactly alike

56.	56.	56.
Attorney V. Torres	Attorney V. Torres	Attorney V. Torres
VTL Section 37-389	VTL Section 37-389	VTL Section 37-389
Location AB29-5853	*Location AR29-5853*	Location AR29-5853
(719) 487-9074 X 32	(719) 487-9074 X 32	(719) 487-9074 X 32
57.	57.	57.
987698935673 - 12	987698935673 - 12	987698935673 - 12
2749 Furley Blvd. 76-89	2749 Furley Blvd. 76-89	2749 Furly Blvd. 76-89
Monroe Ave.	Monroe Ave.	Monroe Ave.
Jenkins & Tyne, PC	Jenkins & Tyne, PC	Jenkins & Tyne, PC
58.	58.	58.
(1) 983-497-3788	(1) 983-497-3738	(1) 983-497-3788
Files 38962-38998	Files 38962-38998	Files 38962-38998
3/5/2419, 4/18/19	**3/5/2419, 4/18/19**	3/5/2419, 4/18/19
CCA Catherine Best	CCA Catherine Best	CCA Catherine West
59.	59.	59.
2806 East 16th St.	2806 East 16th St.	2806 East 16th St.
Dr. Matthew West	Dr. Matthew West	Dr. Matthew West
Civil or Criminal Ct.	Civil or Criminal Ct.	**Civil or Criminal Ct.**
Military Calendar 3	Military Calendar 3	Military Calendar 3
60.	60.	60.
Friday attendance	Friday attendance	Friday attendance
Crim. docket D-2598	Crim. docket D-2598	Crim. docket D-2598
Queens L&T cases	Queens L&T cases	*Queens L&T cases*
File bins F1 and F9	File bins F1 and F9	File bins F7 and F9

Questions 61-75: Record Keeping

"Directions: Answer the fifteen questions based on the information contained in the following tables. Remember, all of the information needed to answer the questions correctly can be found in the tables. Complete the "Daily Breakdown of Cases" and "Summary of Cases" tables before you attempt to answer any of the questions."*

"Part" means Courtroom

"Date Filed" is date the first papers of the case were filed with the clerk of the court.

"Status" means the status of the case at the end of the court session.

"Money Award" means the amount of money that was awarded on that case. The money is
    usually awarded to the party seeking money damages and is paid by the party who was sued.

Daily List of Cases Monday			Table 1
Part	**Date Filed**	**Status of Case**	**Money Award**
Part C	04/09/17	Settled	X
Part A	11/05/18	Dismissed	X
Part B	05/10/17	Defaulted	X
Part C	04/19/18	Settled	$ 8,500
Part A	05/16/18	Adjourned	X
Part D	07/06/18	Dismissed	X
Part B	08/07/18	Adjourned	X
Part C	08/10/19	Settled	$ 11,600
Part A	05/09/19	Defaulted	X
Part B	08/28/19	Adjourned	X
Part D	04/13/19	Settled	$ 14,900
Part C	06/29/19	Adjourned	X
Part A	08/09/19	Settled	$ 13,000

Daily List of Cases Tuesday			Table 2
Part	**Date Filed**	**Status of Case**	**Money Award**
Part D	02/01/17	Defaulted	X
Part A	05/04/17	Settled	X
Part B	03/07/17	Adjourned	X
Part C	04/25/17	Settled	$ 13,900
Part D	05/21/18	Settled	$ 13,700
Part B	07/12/18	Dismissed	X
Part C	10/28/18	Defaulted	X
Part D	11/24/18	Settled	X
Part A	07/12/18	Adjourned	X
Part D	07/26/19	Settled	$ 16,200
Part C	09/22/19	Dismissed	X
Part A	10/22/19	Defaulted	X
Part C	12/18/19	Dismissed	X
Part B	12/24/19	Settled	$ 21,200
Part A	12/11/19	Adjourned	X
Part B	12/18/19	Settled	X

Daily List of Cases Wednesday			Table 3
Part	**Date Filed**	**Status of Case**	**Money Award**
Part A	02/08/17	Dismissed	X
Part C	07/11/17	Settled	X
Part B	10/13/17	Defaulted	X
Part D	11/24/17	Settled	X
Part C	12/11/18	Adjourned	X
Part B	03/05/18	Dismissed	X
Part B	03/11/18	Defaulted	X
Part C	05/22/18	Settled	$14,700
Part D	06/09/18	Adjourned	X
Part B	07/16/19	Adjourned	X
Part B	09/10/19	Settled	$ 19,500
Part C	11/15/19	Adjourned	X
Part D	04/21/19	Settled	$ 16,500
Part A	02/13/19	Dismissed	X
Part D	04/19/19	Defaulted	X
Part A	07/08/19	Settled	$ 13,600

					Table 5
Summary of Cases from Monday, Tuesday, Wednesday					
	Case Status at End of Day				
Part	**Adjourned**	**Defaulted**	**Dismissed**	**Settled With Money Award**	**Settled No Money Award**	**Total Cases**
A						
B						
C						
D						

Status of Case	Monday	Tuesday	Wednesday	Total Cases
Daily Analysis of Cases: Monday, Tuesday, Wednesday				Table 4
Adjourned				
Defaulted				
Dismissed				
Settled - with Money Award				
Settled- with No Money Award				
Total Cases				
Cases by Year Filed				
2017				
2018				
2019				
Total Cases				

Questions 61-75

61. What is the total number of cases adjourned for the three days?

A. 10   C. 12

B. 11   D. none of the above

62. The number of cases "Settled with money award" exceeds the total number of cases "Settled - with no money award" by what number?

A. 4   C. 7

B. 5   D. 6

63. The total number of cases on Tuesday and Wednesday that were filed in 2017 is ___.

A. 4   C. 8

B. 6   D. 10

64. For the three days, what is the total number of adjourned cases plus defaulted cases?

    A. 17   C. 19

    B. 18   D. 20

65. For the three days, what is the total number of cases that were filed in 2018?

    A. 15   C. 17

    B. 16   D. none of the above

66. Which two parts tied for the total number of cases that appeared in their part?

    A. Parts A and D   C. Parts B and C

    B. Parts A and B   D. none of the above

67. Which part had the greatest number of adjourned cases?

    A. Part A   C. Part C

    B. Part B   D. Part D

68. The number of cases on Tuesday exceeds the number of cases on Monday by what number?

    A. 1   C. 3

    B. 2   D. 4

69. Which "Case Status at End of Day" category had the greatest total number of cases for the three days?

    A. Adjourned   C. Defaulted

    B. Dismissed   D. Settled - with Money Award

70. How many 2018 cases were on the Tuesday calendar?

    A. 4   C. 6

    B. 5   D. 3

71. What is the total number of cases in Part C for the three days that were "Settled with money award"?

    A. 3   C. 5

    B. 4   D. 6

72. What is the total number of 2019 cases that appeared on the calendars on Monday and Wednesday?

A. 13   C. 14

B. 12   D. none of the above

73. What is the total number of cases that were dismissed during the three days?

A. 7   C. 5

B. 8   D. 6

74. The total number of adjourned cases exceeded the total number of defaulted cases by___.

A. 1   C. 3

B. 2   D. 4

75. The total number of cases for the three days exceeded the total number of 2017 cases by ____.

A. 25   C. 35

B. 30   D. 34

END OF QUESTIONS FOR PRACTICE TEST 4

ANSWERS: PRACTICE TEST 4

1. C. Ellen Spivek	6. B. Summons Part	11. B. two days
2. D. December 2, 2019	7. B. Thursday	12. C. seven
3. B. West End Avenue	8. A. 2:00 p.m.	13. C. three
4. C. one hour	9. C. Family Court	14. A. Chief Clerk's
5. D. Thursday and Friday	10. B. main electrical panel	15. C. in the basement

16. d. a (singular, to agree with "community")

17. b. jurisdiction (correct spelling)

18. c. associated (logic of sentence)

19. b. services (plural, to agree with "certain")

20. d. income (logic of sentence)

21. d. body (logic of sentence)

22. b. juries (logic of sentence)

23. c. criminal (logic of sentence, to agree with "crimes" mentioned further on in the passage)

24. d. has (correct grammar and logic)

25. b. crimes (logic of sentence)

26. d. allegiance (correct spelling)

27. c. religious (correct spelling)

28. b. acknowledge (correct spelling)

29. d. successful (correct spelling)

30. b. committed (correct spelling)

31. D. She is authorized to file a family court petition for child support because she is an unemancipated child.

32. C. Refer the person to the Summary of Law: "Who May File a Petition for Child Support? and then refer him to the clerk at the petition counter.

33. C. The paper is not proper according to CPLR 2101 because it must be in the English language.

34. C. The exhibit can be filed because it meets the size requirements.

35. D. complaints (is not listed as an exception)

36. D. Venue is the time at which a court session is held. (Venue is the <u>place</u> where a court is held.)

37. C. A person accused of a crime must be present before the court. (This is not correct because "...the rights of those accused of a crime include the right to <u>present a defense</u> before a court.")

38. C. The Traditions of Law in the Western World (Best title. The other titles only refer to sections of the passage.)

39. D. Common law is based upon Roman Law. ("<u>Civil</u> law courts are profoundly based upon Roman Law.")

40. D. Civil law and common law are usually used in different jurisdictions. ("This legal tradition (common law) is practiced in the English and American legal systems...Civil law...became a foundation for university legal education starting in Bologna, Spain and subsequently being taught throughout continental European Universities.)

41. Choice D: if all the sets are exactly alike.

42. Choice A: if none of the three sets are exactly alike
    2871 Westminster St.   2871 Westminster St.   2871 **East**minster St.
    Ct. Rep. Abrantes   Ct. Rep. Abran**tis**   Ct. Rep. Abrantes

43. Choice B: if only the second and third sets are exactly alike
    Martin S. **C**oltun   Martin S. Colton   Martin S. Colton

44. Choice C: if only the first and second sets are exactly alike
    37421253832-4439   37421253832-4439   37421253832-44**36**

45. Choice C: if only the first and second sets are exactly alike

    (856) 386-9375 Ext. 2   (856) 386-9375 Ext. 2   (856) 386-9375 Ext. **5**

46. Choice A: if all the sets are exactly alike.

47. Choice D: if none of the three sets are exactly alike

    973689036552-38   973689036552-38   97368903**652**-38

    1641 Kings Avenue   1641 **King** Avenue   1641 Kings Avenue

48. Choice B: if only the second and third sets are exactly alike

    Files 45593-**485**93   Files 45593-448593   Files 45593-448593

49. Choice C: if only the first and second sets are exactly alike

    849297753978   849297753978   849297753**798**

50. Choice C: if only the first and second sets are exactly alike

    Fernando Devine   Fernando Devine   Ferna**nde** Devine

51. Choice D: if none of the three sets are exactly alike

    Referee Hartman   Referee Hartman   Referee Hart**men**

    Lora S. Martinoff   Lora S. Mart**inof**   Lora S. Martinoff

52. Choice A: if only the first and second sets are exactly alike

    Statute 2757-12669   Statute 2757-12669   Statu**tes** 2757-1266

53. Choice C: if all the sets are exactly alike

54. Choice B: if only the second and third sets are exactly alike

    OCL Juanita Davila   OCI Juanita Davila   OCI Juanita Davila

55. Choice A: if only the first and second sets are exactly alike

    Carla D. Benevento   Carla D. Benevento   Carla D. Be**niv**ento

56. Choice A: if only the second and third sets are exactly alike

    Location **AB2**9-5853   Location AR29-5853   Location AR29-5853

57. Choice B: if only the first and second sets are exactly alike

    2749 Furley Blvd.   2749 Furley Blvd.   2749 Fu**rly** Blvd.

58. Choice D: if none of the three sets are exactly alike

    (1) 983-497-3788   (1) 983-497-3**738**   (1) 983-497-3788

    CCA Catherine Best   CCA Catherine Best   CCA Catherine **We**st

59. Choice C: if all the sets are exactly alike.

60. Choice B: if only the first and second sets are exactly alike

File bins F1 and F9   File bins F1 and F9   File bins **F7** and F9

Status of Case	Monday		Tuesday		Wednesday		Total Cases
		Table 4					
Adjourned	llll	4	lll	3	llll	4	11
Defaulted	ll	2	lll	3	lll	3	8
Dismissed	ll	2	lll	3	lll	3	8
Settled - with Money Award	llll	4	llll	4	llll	4	12
Settled- with No Money Award	l	1	lll	3	ll	2	6
Total Cases		13		16		16	45
Cases by Year Filed							
2017	ll	2	llll	4	llll	4	10
2018	lllll	5	lllll	5	lllll	5	15
2019	lllll l	6	lllll ll	7	lllll ll	7	20
Total Cases		13		16		16	45

Table 4 — Daily Analysis of Cases: Monday, Tuesday and Wednesday

Table 5 — Summary of Cases from Monday, Tuesday and Wednesday

Part	Adjourned		Defaulted		Dismissed		Settled With Money Award		Settled No Money Award		Total Cases
A	lll	3	ll	2	lll	3	ll	2	l	1	11
B	llll	4	lll	3	ll	2	ll	2	l	1	12
C	lll	3	l	1	ll	2	llll	4	ll	2	12
D	l	1	ll	2	l	1	llll	4	ll	2	10
		11		8		8		12		6	45

61. B. 11

62. D. 6 (12 - 6 = 6)

63. C. 8 (4 + 4 = 8)

64. C. 19 (11 + 8 = 19)

65. A. 15

66. C. Parts B and C (each handled 12 cases)

67. B. Part B (4 cases)

68. C. 3 (16 - 13 = 3)

69. D. Settled - with Money Award (12 cases)

70. B. 5

71. B. 4

72. A. 13 (6 + 7 = 13)

73. B. 8

74. C. 3 (11 - 8 = 3)

75. C. 35 (45 - 10 = 35)

END OF ANSWERS FOR PRACTICE TEST 4

PRACTICE TEST 5: QUESTIONS
(75 Questions: Time allowed: 3.5 hours)

Questions 1-15: Remembering Facts and Information

"Directions: Read the brief story below. Study it for five minutes. Then, turn the story over and wait for ten minutes before you answer the fifteen questions on the following page. Try to remember as many details of the incident without making any written notes."*

(Written test: At the end of the five minutes, the test monitor will collect this sheet and ten minutes after that, you will be instructed to begin the test by answering from memory the first fifteen questions relating to this story.

Computer test: At the end of the five minutes, the passage will disappear from the screen and ten minutes after that, you will be instructed to begin the test by answering from memory the first fifteen questions relating to this story.)

On September 14, 2019, Court Officers Janice Baranov and Max Chang were both assigned to the Supreme Court, Civil Term, Part 19C at the Supreme Court of New York County, located at 27 Leighman Street. They were scheduled to fill-in for two Court Officers (Court Officer Bryan Woods and Court Officer Wilma Faulkner) that were requalifying with their firearms (Glock 19) on that day. Although it was their first day assigned to the Part, it was the last day of a trial that had been going on for the preceding 12 court days. Summations by the attorneys had been completed the previous day, as had the Judge's directions to the jury. A final attempt by Judge Clarkson to settle the dispute had resulted in a proposed settlement that required the disposition of two cases in other courts involving the parties.

One case was a civil case that was on the NYC Civil Court calendar. The second case was a criminal case that was on the NYC Criminal Court calendar. Although both case profiles were in the court database, some of the most recent orders and exhibits were not. Because of this, Court Officer Janice Baranov picked up the case file at NYC Civil Court and Court Officer Chang picked up the criminal court case file at the NYC Criminal Court.

Both cases were reviewed by Judge Clarkson and the two attorneys. After a conference lasting one hour, they agreed on dispositions for both cases and the Supreme Court case. The criminal court disposition was approved by the judge after a call to the assigned ADA. By 3:00 p.m., a written settlement had been signed by both parties and the Judge. At 3:30 p.m., the Judge informed the jury of the settlement. He thanked them for their service, and released them from the case.

On the following pages there are 15 questions. Answer the questions based on the information provided in the preceding passage.

1. On what date did the events of the preceding passage occur?

A. September 4, 2019   C. September 24, 2019

B. September 14, 2019   D. none of the above

2. What is the first name of Officer Chang?

A. Martin   C. Morris

B. Max   D. none of the above

3. What is the last name of the Judge?

A. Clarke   C. Clarkson

B. Claridon   D. none of the above

4. The type of firearm that the two Court Officers were going to requalify on was a _____ 19.

A. Colt   C. Couger

B. Glock   D. none of the above

5. The address of the Supreme Court building is 27 _____ Street.

A. Larchmont   C. Lemmings

B. Larson   D. Leighman

6. The criminal court disposition was approved by the judge after a call to the assigned _____.

A. ABA   C. AD

B. ADA   D. AD

7. How long did the afternoon conference last?

A. half an hour   C. two hours

B. one hour   D. none of the above

8. What is the first name of Court Officer Baranov?

A. Alice   C. Janice

B. Eliza   D. none of the above

9. The passage deals with Supreme Court, Civil Term, Part _____.

A. 9B   C. 9C

B. 19B   D. 19C

10. By _____ p.m., a written settlement had been signed by both parties.

A. 2:00   C. 2:30

B. 3:00   D. none of the above

11. Before the events in this passage, the trial had been going on for the previous _____ court days.

A. 10   C. 12

B. 11   D. none of the above

12. At which court did Court Officer Baranov pick up a case file?

A. Supreme Court   C. NYC Criminal Court

B. NYC Civil Court   D. NYS Court of Claims

13. At what time did the Judge release the jury from the case?

A. 3:30 p.m.   C. 3:00 p.m.

B. 2:30 p.m.   D. none of the above

14. Although both case profiles were in the court database, some of the most recent _____ and exhibits were not.

A. complaints   C. judgments

B. EBTs   D. orders

15. In what county is the Supreme Court located?

A. Kings County   C. New York County

B. Queens County   D. none of the above

▲

Questions 16 - 35: Reading, Understanding and Interpreting Written Material

"Directions: The three passages below each contain five numbered blanks. Below each passage are listed five sets of words numbered to match the blanks. Pick the word from each set which seems to make the most sense both in the sentence and the total paragraph."*

Passage 1

"The history of crowd control starts back in the 1920s, when there was no official ___16___ control unit. There would be ten to 20 officers lined up. Behind ___17___ line there would be another line about twenty feet back. The ___18___ were armed with ___19___ and axe handles. Their job is to simply hold the crowd back, which would just end in a free for all and resulting in multiple officer injuries. Later in the 1950s the first actual riot control teams armed with riot shields and batons. The goal was for the riot shield ___20___ to hold up the lines. When they came to actual contact with the crowd the officers with the batons were supposed to help the riot shield officers. However if deadly forced was used against them there was no training or procedure to counter this. The officers at this point were left to fend for themselves."[1]

16.	17.	18.	19.	20.
a. rules	a. several	a. crowd	a. botons	a. officer
b. individual	b. one	b. perpetrators	b. batons	b. officers
c. personal	c. two	c. officers	c. bottons	c. patrolman
d. crowd	d. many	d. criminals	d. battons	d. soldier

Passage 2

"The "petit jury" (or "trial jury", sometimes "petty jury") hears the evidence in a trial as presented by both the ___21___ (petitioner) and the defendant (respondent). ___22___ hearing the evidence and often jury instructions from the judge, the group ___23___ for deliberation, to consider a verdict. The majority required for a verdict ___24___. In some cases it must be unanimous, while in other jurisdictions it may be a ___25___ or supermajority. A jury that is unable to come to a verdict is referred to as a hung jury. The size of the jury varies; in criminal cases involving serious felonies there are usually 12 jurors."(1)

21.	22.	23.	24.	25.
a. plaintaff	a. before	a. depart	a. veries	a. minority
b. plaintiff	b. prior	b. retreat	b. varies	b. part
c. plaintaf	c. after	c. recede	c. verries	c. majority
d. plaintif	d. previously	d. retires	d. varries	d. few

Passage 3

"In the United States, court dockets are considered to be ___26___ records, and many public records databases and directories include ___27___ to court dockets. Rules of civil procedure often state that the court clerk shall record certain information "on the docket" when ___28___ specific event occurs. The Federal Courts use the PACER (Public Access Court Electronic Records) system to house dockets and documents on all federal civil, criminal and ___29___ cases, available to the public for a fee. The term ___30___ also sometimes used informally to refer to a court calendar, the schedule of the appearances, arguments and/or hearings scheduled for a court. It may also be used as a metonym to refer to a court's caseload as a whole. Thus, either sense may be intended (depending upon the context) in the frequent use of the phrase "crowded dockets" by legal journalists and commentators.(1)

26.	27.	28.	29.	30.
a. private	a. refrinces	a. two	a. bankruptsy	a. are
b. secret	b. refferances	b. several	b. bankruptsi	b. were
c. person	c. references	c. a	c. bankruptcy	c. is
d. public	d. reffrenses	d. many	d. bankruptcies	d. aren't

Questions 31 - 35: Applying Facts and Information to Given Situations

"Directions: Use the information preceding each question to answer the question. Only that information should be used in answering the questions. Do not use any prior knowledge you may have on the subject. Choose the alternative that best answers the question."*

Question 31 and 32

Screening Procedure

All individuals who wish to enter the courthouse must submit to security screening. Individuals who refuse to submit to security screening shall not be allowed to enter the courthouse.

All individuals shall be processed through the metal detectors according to the following procedure:

1. All bags and personal belongings (purses, jewelry, watches, backpacks, and pocket contents, etc.) must be placed on the x-ray belt.
2. Overcoats and jackets shall also be scanned on the x-ray machine.
3. All persons must walk through the metal detector.

If the metal detector sets off an alarm, a Court Officer may perform another scan with a hand-held wand. The Court Officer may also conduct a physical search of any or all personal articles to determine the reason for the alarm.

Situation 1

Attorney Sylvia Samuelson, who is well known to Court Officer Lorna Vasillo, went through the screening procedure at 9:08 a.m., when she first entered the courthouse. At 10:02 a.m. she walked out of the courthouse to retrieve a document from her parked car. Upon returning to the courthouse entrance at 10:08 a.m., she spoke with Court Officer Vasillo and asked that she be permitted to skip the screening because she was in a hurry to get back to her courtroom, where a calendar call was in progress.

31. Based on the above procedure and situation 1, which of the following choices is the best course of action that Court Officer Vasillo should take?

A. Allow the attorney to skip the screening because she had been screened earlier in the morning.

B. Allow the attorney to skip the screening because she is known to the Court Officer.

C. Allow the attorney to skip the screening because the calendar call was underway and she needed to get to the courtroom quickly.

D. Inform the attorney that she must be screened.

Situation 2

As attorney Kevin Dougon walks through the metal detector, an alarm goes off. The attorney quickly states that he forgot to remove his phone from his pants pocket.

32. Choose the best answer:

Based on the preceding rule and situation 2, what is Court Officer Vasillo required to do?

A. perform another scan with a hand-held wand

B. conduct a physical search of any or all personal articles

C. perform another scan with a hand-held wand and conduct a physical search of any or all personal articles

D. none of the above

Questions 33 - 35

ADA Service Animal Guidelines

"The ADA provides explicit coverage for service animals. Guidelines have been developed not only to protect persons with disabilities, but also to indemnify businesses from damages related to granting access to service animals on their premises. Businesses are allowed to ask if the animal is a service animal and ask what tasks it is trained to perform, but they are not allowed to ask the service animal to perform the task nor ask for a special ID of the animal. They cannot ask what the person's disabilities are. A person with a disability cannot be removed from the premises unless either of two things happen: the animal is out of control and its owner cannot get it under control (e.g. a dog barking uncontrollably in a restaurant), or the animal is a direct threat to people's health and safety. Allergies and fear of animals would not be considered a threat to people's health and safety, so it would not be a valid reason to deny access to people with service animals. Businesses that prepare or serve food must allow service animals and their owners on the premises even if state or local health laws otherwise prohibit animals on the premises. In this case, businesses that prepare or serve food are not required to provide care or food for service animals, nor do they have to provide a designated area for the service animal to relieve itself. Lastly, people that require service dogs cannot be charged an extra fee for their service dog or be treated unfairly, for example, being isolated from people at a restaurant. People with disabilities cannot be treated as "less than" other customers. However, if a business normally charges for damages caused by the person to property, the customer with a disability will be charged for his/her service animal's damages to the property."(1)

Situation

Court Officer Bruce Forester is staffing the security station at the front entrance of the Criminal Court building when a man enters with a German Shepherd dog. The man seems very physically fit and alert. He informs Court Officer Forester that the dog is a "service animal" and that they both will be going to Criminal Court Part 7 where a trial is being held.

33. Based on the above "ADA Service Animal Guidelines" and Situation for question 33, which of the following is a proper action for Court Officer Forester to take?
A. Ask the person if the animal is really a service animal and where it was trained.
B. Deny entry of the animal due to the fact that the person appears physically and mentally fit.
C. Ask what tasks the service animal is trained to perform.
D. Inquire as to what the person's disabilities are so that a determination can be made.

34. Based on the above "ADA Service Animal Guidelines" and Situation for question 33, which of the following is a proper action for Court Officer Forester to take?
A. Ask that the service animal to perform a task to prove that it is really a service animal.
B. Immediately remove the person and the animal from the premises.
C. Ask if the animal is a service animal.
D. Deny entry of the service animal if doing so would be contrary to local and state law.

35. Based on the above "ADA Service Animal Guidelines" and Situation for question 33:
A. Every service animal may be treated differently, according to the size of the animal.
B. Service animals do not include ducks.
C. A service animal must wear an identifying tag around its neck.
D. A person with disabilities may under certain circumstances be removed from the premises.

For questions 36 - 40, read the passage and then answer the questions based solely on the information provided in the passage.

Passage for questions 36-38

The role of the emergency nurse is to evaluate and monitor patients and to manage their care in the emergency department. They also may supervise unlicensed assistive personnel ("nurse aides" or "care partners"). It can be a challenge to get everything done quickly and correctly in an ever-changing environment. Some ED nurse functions are common to other nursing specialties, while others are specific to emergency nursing. These can be divided into 1) assessment, 2) planning and managing care, 3) tasks, 4) communication, and 5) teaching.

Assessment. Emergency nurses interview a patient to get a health history, a list of current medications being taken and allergies. He or she performs a physical examination. This is often a limited exam based on the patient's chief complaint and only infrequently a complete head-to-toe examination. The ED nurse periodically reassesses the patient to detect any changes, either improvement, decompensation or no change. This may be done after a treatment is given to evaluate its effectiveness or at certain time intervals as appropriate for the patient's condition.

Planning and managing care. The ED nurse must have a plan of what to do for the patient, when and in what order. Managing an ED patient's care includes decisions such as whether the patient can go to X ray before getting blood drawn, what tasks to delegate to unlicensed assistive personnel (UAPs), and how many visitors are allowed in the patient's room, among others.

36. According to the preceding passage, which of the following statements is not correct?

A. An ED nurse may decide how many visitors are allowed in the patient's room.

B. The ED nurse may supervise unlicensed assistive personnel.

C. An ED nurse may interview a patient to get a health history.

D. The ED nurse performs a mental examination.

37. Which of the following statements is not supported by the preceding passage?

A. The ED nurse must have a plan of what to do for the patient.

B. The ED nurse may supervise nurse aides.

C. Almost all ED nurses are female.

D. The ED nurse may decide on the order of medical treatment.

38. Which of the following statements is not supported by the preceding passage?

A. ED nurses work in the emergency department.

B. The ED nurse must have a plan as to what to do with the patient.

C. The ED nurse periodically reassesses the patient.

D. The ED nurse always performs a complete medical examination.

Passage for questions 39-40

Clerical workers are perhaps the largest occupational group in the United States. In 2004, there were 3.1 million general office clerks, 1.5 million office administrative supervisors and 4.1 million secretaries. Clerical occupations often do not require a college degree, though some college education or 1 to 2 years in vocational programs are common qualifications. Familiarity with office equipment and certain software programs is also often required. Employers may provide clerical training. The median salary for clerks is $23,000, while the national median income for workers age 25 or older is $33,000. Median salaries ranged from $22,770 for general office clerks to $34,970 for secretaries and $41,030 for administrative supervisors. Clerical workers are considered working class by American sociologists such as William Thompson, Joseph Hickey or James Henslin as they perform highly routinized tasks with relatively little autonomy. Sociologist Dennis Gilbert, argues that the white and blue collar divide has shifted to a divide between professionals, including some semi-professionals, and routinized white collar workers. White collar office supervisors may be considered lower middle class with some secretaries being located in that part of the socio-economic strata where the working and middle classes overlap.

Traditionally clerical positions have been held almost exclusively by women. Even today, the vast majority of clerical workers in the US continue to be female. As with other predominantly female positions, clerical occupations were, and to some extent continue to be, assigned relatively low prestige on a sexist basis. The term pink-collar worker is often used to describe predominantly female white collar positions.

39. According to the preceding passage:

A. Clerical occupations often require a college degree.

B. The median salary for clerks is $33,000

C. White collar office supervisors may be considered upper middle class.

D. Women have traditionally held most clerical positions.

40. Which of the following statements is supported by the above passage? The total "clerical workers" mentioned in the preceding passage is:

A. 5.6 million   C. 8.7 million

B. 3.1 million   D. none of the above

Questions 41-60: Clerical Checking

Directions: The following example consists of five sets of information. Compare the information in the three sets, and on your answer sheet, mark:

Choice A: if none of the three sets are exactly alike

Choice B: if only the second and third sets are exactly alike

Choice C: if only the first and second sets are exactly alike

Choice D: if all the sets are exactly alike.

41. JHO C. Alderman MHL 95.05 (d - e) **4279-29 3rd Avenue** Records 5069: T3782	41. JHO C. Alderman *MHL 95.05 (d - e)* 4279-29 3rd Avenue Records 5069: T3782	41. JHO C. Alderman MHL 95.05 (d - e) 4279-29 3rd Avenue Records 5069: T3782
42. TSF: 6/14/19 - S-T 2893 East Oak St. Ct. Int. Velazquez Monroe, PA 21297	42. TSF: 6/14/19 - S-T 2893 East Oak St. Ct. Int. Velazquez Monvoe, PA 21297	42. TSF: 6/14/19 - S-T 2898 East Oak St. Ct. Int. Velazquez Monroe, PA 21297
43. PL 4364 S. 324.14 Larry Hellier, JHO COT 4745/2020 9/1 K. Ingers - Ref. 6633	43. PL 4364 S. 324.14 Larry Heller, JHO COT 4745/2020 9/1 K. Ingers - Ref. 6633	43. PL 4364 S. 324.14 *Larry Heller, JHO* COT 4745/2020 9/1 K. Ingers - Ref. 6633
44. Elway and Monalsco 47178462-269592 364-672-3573 (NJ) CPL 5520:21 (a - z)	44. Elway and Monalsco 471783462-269592 364-672-3573 (NJ) **CPL 5520:21 (a - z)**	44. Elway and Monalsco 471783462-269592 364-672-3573 (NJ) CPL 5520:21 (a - z)
45. Nancy Bushneller *Support Order 20F* CA Jenny Chan 783956450396 - 39	45. Nancy Bushneller Support Order 20F CA Jenny Chan 783956450396 - 39	45. Nancy Bushneller **Support Order 20F** CA Jenny Chen 783956450396 - 39

Directions: The following example consists of five sets of information. Compare the information in the three sets, and on your answer sheet, mark:

Choice A: if all the sets are exactly alike.

Choice B: if only the second and third sets are exactly alike

Choice C: if only the first and second sets are exactly alike

Choice D: if none of the three sets are exactly alike

46. Ref. Edward Blaynes VTL & MHL 2019/20 Placard D85894 DIS John Francis Bolman	46. Ref. Edward Blaynes VTL & MHL 2019/20 Placard D85894 DIS John **Francis Bolman**	46. Ref. Edward Blaynes VTL & MHL 2019/20 Placard D85894 DIS John Francis Bolmen
47. 86489630986 GKOC *6461 Barrister Rd.* (985) 284-8749 X 9 Furman & Damin, PC	47. 86489630986 GKOC 6461 Barrister Rd. (985) 284-8749 X 6 Furman & Damin, PC	47. 86489630986 GKOC 6461 Barister Rd. *(985) 284-8749 X 9* Furman & Damin, PC
48. Kursted Blvd., East Files 38892-438759 **7/11/2019, 8/25/19** Witness W. Damien	48. Kursted Blvd., East Files 38892-438759 7/11/2019, 8/25/19 Witness M. Damien	48. Kursted Blvd., East Files 38892-438759 7/11/2019, 8/25/19 Witness M. Damien
49. Parts 44B, 48A, 25D JHO Boris K. Vasiliof Nassau and Suffolk Niagara Falls 2020	49. Parts 44B, 48A, 25D JHO Boris K. Vasiliof *Nassau and Suffolk* Niagara Falls 2020	49. Parts 44B, 48A, 25D JHO Boris K. Vasiliof Nassau and Suffolk Niagara Falls 2020
50. Village Road West Bernardo Fontarro Ref. Numb. 658315 FC File H-3876/19	50. Village Road West Bernardo Fontarro Ref. Numb. 658315 FC File H-3876/19	50. Village Road West **Bernardo Fontaro** Ref. Numb. 658315 FC File H-3876/19

Directions: The following example consists of five sets of information. Compare the information in the three sets, and on your answer sheet, mark:

Choice A: if only the first and second sets are exactly alike

Choice B: if only the second and third sets are exactly alike

Choice C: if all the sets are exactly alike.

Choice D: if none of the three sets are exactly alike

51. Interpreter Magellan MHL Amend. 325/19 (749) 865-8463 X 32 Carlos Chin ID 8675	51. Interpreter Magellan MHL Amend. 325/19 **(749) 865-8463 X 32** Carlos Chin ID 8675	51. Interpreter Magellan MHL Amend. 325/19 (749) 865-8463 X 32 Carlos Chin ID 8675
52. Part 24 (5/27/2020) *2872 North Elmont* Divisions A and C Lima & Traynor, PC	52. Part 24 (5/27/2020) 2872 North Elmont Divisions A and C Lima & Traynor, PC	52. Part 24 (5/27/2020) 2872 North Ellmont Divisions A and C Lima & Traynor, PC
53. 759111897863 - 78 Files 34693-994122 9/15/2019, 10/25/19 Captain G. Frement	53. 759111897863 - 78 *Files 34693-994122* 9/15/2019, 10/25/19 Captain G. Frementi	53. 759111897863 - 78 Files 34693-994122 9/15/2019, 10/25/19 **Captain G. Frementi**
54. Parts 37M, 32C, 48D Judge John D. Wang Little Pond Road N. 763-378-4679 Ext. 5	54. Parts 37M, 32C, 48C Judge John D. Wang Little Pond Road N. 763-378-4679 Ext. 5	54. Parts 37M, 32C, 48C Judge John B. Wang Little Pond Road N. 763-378-4679 Ext. 5
55. Nassau Section 1354 Loretta S. Johnson **Ref. Numb. 6967462** FC File S-25784/19	55. Nassau Section 1354 Loretta S. Johnson Ref. Numb. 6967462 FC File S-25784/19	55. Nassau Section 1354 *Loreta S. Johnson* Ref. Numb. 6967462 FC File S-25784/19

Directions: The following example consists of five sets of information. Compare the information in the three sets, and on your answer sheet, mark:

Choice A: if only the second and third sets are exactly alike

Choice B: if only the first and second sets are exactly alike

Choice C: if all the sets are exactly alike.

Choice D: if none of the three sets are exactly alike

56. Expert Witness #4 75639773524 - B LicenseMKSA4J99D **Richard Laurelton**	56. Expert Witness #4 756397773524 - B LicenseMKSA4J99D Richard Laurelton	56. Expert Witness #4 756397773524 - B LicenseMKSA4J99D Richard Laurelton
57. *Parts 12B and 16D)* 5893 Woodward Ln. Sect. BU6442: 87514 876 87876 5649 909	57. Parts 12B and 16D) 5893 Woodward Ln. Sect. BU6442: 87514 876 87876 5649 909	57. Parts 12B and 16D) 5893 Woodward Ln. Sect. BU6442: 87514 876 87876 5646 909
58. (1) 873-294-4778 Files 38972-39432 9/11/2419, 10/24/19 CO Brenda Byrnes	58. (1) 873-294-4778 Files 38972-39432 9/11/2419, 10/24/19 CO Brenda Burnes	58. (1) 873-294-4778 **Files 38972-39342** 9/11/2419, 10/24/19 CO Brenda Byrnes
59. 3717 West 13th Ave. Official Interpreter Civil or Family Court Ready Calendar 2	59. 3717 West 18th Ave. *Official Interpreter* Civil or Family Court Ready Calendar 2	59. 3717 West 18th Ave. Official Interpreter Civil or Family Court Ready Calendar 2
60. Friday Morning Cal. Crim. docket D-7547 **Donner Hill Road** Locations E2-F20	60. Friday Morning Cal. Crim. docket D-7547 Donner Hill Road Locations E2-F20	60. Friday Morning Cal. Crim. docket D-7547 *Doaner Hill Road* Locations E2-F20

Questions 61-75: Record Keeping

"Directions: Answer the fifteen questions based on the information contained in the following tables. Remember, all of the information needed to answer the questions correctly can be found in the tables. Complete the "Daily Breakdown of Cases" and "Summary of Cases" tables before you attempt to answer any of the questions."*

"Part" means Courtroom

"Date Filed" is date the first papers of the case were filed with the clerk of the court.

"Status" means the status of the case at the end of the court session.

"Money Award" means the amount of money that was awarded on that case. The money is usually awarded to the party seeking money damages and is paid by the party who was sued.

Table 1: Daily List of Cases Monday			
Part	**Date Filed**	**Status of Case**	**Money Award**
Part D	07/07/17	Defaulted	X
Part A	08/04/18	Settled	$12,400
Part C	09/06/17	Adjourned	X
Part B	04/21/19	Dismissed	X
Part A	06/15/18	Adjourned	X
Part D	08/10/17	Dismissed	X
Part A	08/16/18	Adjourned	X
Part B	10/21/19	Settled	$18,700
Part D	09/17/18	Dismissed	X
Part B	03/09/19	Settled	X
Part C	05/12/19	Adjourned	X
Part B	07/09/19	Settled	X
Part A	09/22/19	Settled	$19,200

Table 2: Daily List of Cases Tuesday			
Part	**Date Filed**	**Status of Case**	**Money Award**
Part D	08/06/17	Defaulted	X
Part A	07/05/18	Adjourned	X
Part C	10/05/17	Settled	$16,700
Part B	06/19/19	Adjourned	X
Part A	08/17/18	Settled	X
Part D	10/02/17	Dismissed	X
Part A	01/18/18	Adjourned	X
Part B	02/19/19	Settled	X
Part D	03/28/18	Dismissed	X
Part C	06/14/18	Settled	$19,300
Part B	08/15/18	Defaulted	X
Part A	09/12/18	Adjourned	X
Part D	02/12/19	Dismissed	X
Part B	04/19/19	Settled	X
Part A	06/21/19	Settled	$13,500
Part C	09/13/19	Defaulted	X

Table 3: Daily List of Cases Wednesday			
Part	**Date Filed**	**Status of Case**	**Money Award**
Part D	10/16/17	Adjourned	X
Part A	05/07/18	Settled	$12,700
Part C	11/03/17	Adjourned	X
Part B	07/18/19	Settled	X
Part A	09/19/18	Adjourned	X
Part D	11/13/17	Dismissed	X
Part B	04/19/18	Settled	$17,200
Part D	02/27/19	Settled	X
Part A	06/22/18	Defaulted	X
Part C	09/13/18	Settled	X
Part B	05/13/19	Dismissed	X
Part A	07/26/19	Adjourned	X
Part C	08/07/19	Settled	X
Part D	09/12/19	Settled	$18,900
Part B	10/22/19	Defaulted	X
Part A	11/07/19	Adjourned	X

Table 4: Daily Analysis of Cases: Monday, Tuesday and Wednesday				
Status of Case	**Monday**	**Tuesday**	**Wednesday**	**Total Cases**
Adjourned				
Defaulted				
Dismissed				
Settled - with Money Award				
Settled- with No Money Award				
Total Cases				
Cases by Year Filed				
2017				
2018				
2019				
Total Cases				

Table 5: Summary of Cases from Monday and Tuesday						
	Case Status at End of Day					
Part	**Adjourned**	**Defaulted**	**Dismissed**	**Settled With Money Award**	**Settled No Money Award**	**Total Cases**
A						
B						
C						
D						
Total						

Questions 61-75

61. Which of the four following categories has the greatest total number of cases?

    A. Adjourned   C. Defaulted

    B. Dismissed   D. Settled - with Money Award

62. The total number of "Dismissed" cases exceeds the total number of "Defaulted" case by_____.

    A. 1   C. 3

    B. 2   D. none of the above

63. What is the total number of cases filed in 2017 and 2019?

    A. 27   C. 29

    B. 28   D. none of the above

64. Which year had the greatest number of cases filed?

    A. 2016   C. 2018

    B. 2017   D. 2019

65. What is the total number of cases for the three days?

    A. 43   C. 45

    B. 46   D. none of the above

66. How many cases were adjourned in Part A for the three days?

    A. 5   C. 6

    B. 7   D. none of the above

67. Which part had the greatest number of "Dismissed" case for the three days?

    A. Part A   C. Part D

    B. Part B   D. none of the above

68. Which part had 3 adjourned cases for the three days?

    A. Part D   C. Part B

    B. Part C   D. Part A

69. What is the total number of cases "Adjourned" and "Defaulted" for the three days?

   A. 16   C. 18

   B. 17   D. none of the above

70. Which part handled the greatest number of cases for the three days?

   A. Part A   C. Part C

   B. Part B   D. Part D

71. Which part had for the three days an equal number of cases "Settled With Money Award" and "Settled With No Money Award??"

   A. Part A   C. Part C

   B. Part B   D. Part D

72. Which year had the least number of cases filed?

   A. 2016   C. 2018

   B. 2017   D. 2019

73. What is the total number of adjourned cases in Part C for the three days?

   A. 5   C. 6

   B. 4   D. none of the above

74. What is the total number for the three days of "Adjourned", "Defaulted" and "Dismissed" cases?

   A. 24   C. 26

   B. 25   D. none of the above

75. Which "Case Status" had the greatest total number of cases for the three days?

   A. Defaulted   C. Adjourned

   B. Dismissed   D. "Settled-With Money Award"

END OF QUESTIONS FOR PRACTICE TEST 5

ANSWERS: PRACTICE TEST 5

1. B. September 14, 2019	6. B. ADA	11. C. 12
2. B. Max	7. B. one hour	12. B. NYC Civil Court
3. C. Clarkson	8. C. Janice	13. A. 3:30 p.m.
4. B. Glock	9. D. 19C	14. D. orders
5. D. Leighman	10. B. 3:00	15. C. New York County

16. d. crowd (to agree with subject of the passage)

17. b. one (grammar: to agree with singular "line")

18. c. officers (logic of sentence)

19. b. batons (correct spelling)

20. b. officers (logic and agreement with plural "they" in the following sentence)

21. b. plaintiff (correct spelling)

22. c. after (logic of sentence)

23. d. retires (singular, for "group")

24. b. varies (correct spelling)

25. c. majority (logic of sentence)

26. d. public (logic of sentence)

27. c. references (correct spelling)

28. c. a (singular "specific event")

29. c. bankruptcy (correct spelling)

30. c. is (to agree with singular "term")

31. D. Inform the attorney that she must be screened. (The procedure states, "All individuals who wish to enter the courthouse must submit to security screening." It does not list any exceptions.)

32. D. none of the above (The procedure states that the Court Officer "MAY perform another scan with a hand-held wand. The Court Officer MAY also conduct a physical search of any or all personal articles to determine the reason for the alarm.")

33. C. Ask what tasks the service animal is trained to perform. ("Businesses are allowed to ask if the animal is a service animal and ask what tasks it is trained to perform.")

34. C. Ask if the animal is a service animal. ("Businesses are allowed to ask if the animal is a service animal and ask what tasks it is trained to perform....")

35. D. A person with disabilities may under certain circumstances be removed from the premises. "A person with a disability cannot be removed from the premises unless either of two things

happen: the animal is out of control and its owner cannot get it under control (e.g. a dog barking uncontrollably in a restaurant), or the animal is a direct threat to people's health and safety.

36. D. The ED nurse performs a mental examination. (This is not correct because according to the passage, "He or she performs a <u>physical</u> examination.")

37. C. Almost all ED nurses are female. (The passage does not mention the percentage of male or female ED nurses.)

38. D. The ED nurse performs always performs a complete medical examination. (This is not supported by the passage. The passage states that the exam"... is often a limited exam based on the patient's chief complaint and only infrequently a complete head-to-toe examination.")

39. D. Women have traditionally held most clerical positions. ("Traditionally clerical positions have been held almost exclusively by women.")

40. C. 8.7 million (3.1 million general office clerks + 1.5 million office administrative supervisors + 4.1 million secretaries = 8.7 million)

41. Choice D: if all the sets are exactly alike.

42. Choice A: if none of the three sets are exactly alike
    2893 East Oak St.   2893 East Oak St.   28**98** East Oak St.
    Monroe, PA 21297   Mon**voe**, PA 21297   Monroe, PA 21297

43. Choice B: if only the second and third sets are exactly alike
    Larry Hel**lier**, JHO   Larry Heller, JHO   Larry Heller, JHO

44. Choice B: if only the second and third sets are exactly alike
    4717**84**62-269592   471783462-269592   471783462-269592

45. Choice C: if only the first and second sets are exactly alike
    CA Jenny Chan   CA Jenny Chan   CA Jenny **Chen**

46. Choice C: if only the first and second sets are exactly alike
    John Francis Bolman   John Francis Bolman   John Francis Bol**men**

47. Choice D: if none of the three sets are exactly alike
    6461 Barrister Rd.   6461 Barrister Rd.   6461 B**aris**ter Rd.
    (985) 284-8749 X 9   (985) 284-8749 **X 6**   (985) 284-8749 X 9

48. Choice B: if only the second and third sets are exactly alike
    Witness **W.** Damien   Witness M. Damien   Witness M. Damien

49. Choice A: if all the sets are exactly alike

50. Choice C: if only the first and second sets are exactly alike
Bernardo Fontarro   Bernardo Fontarro   Bernardo Fon**taro**

51. Choice C: if all the sets are exactly alike.

52. Choice A: if only the first and second sets are exactly alike
2872 North Elmont   2872 North Elmont   2872 North **Ell**mont

53. Choice B: if only the second and third sets are exactly alike
Captain G. Frem**ent**   Captain G. Frementi   Captain G. Frementi

54. Choice D: if none of the three sets are exactly alike
Parts 37M, 32C, **48D**   Parts 37M, 32C, 48C   Parts 37M, 32C, 48C
Judge John D. Wang   Judge John D. Wang   Judge John **B**. Wang

55. Choice A: if only the first and second sets are exactly alike
Loretta S. Johnson   Loretta S. Johnson   Lor**eta** S. Johnson

56. Choice A: if only the second and third sets are exactly alike
7563**977**3524 - B   756397773524 - B   756397773524 - B

57. Choice B: if only the first and second sets are exactly alike
876 87876 5649 909   876 87876 5649 909   876 87876 **5646** 909

58. Choice D: if none of the three sets are exactly alike
Files 38972-39432   Files 38972-39432   Files 38972-39**342**
CO Brenda Byrnes   CO Brenda **Burn**es   CO Brenda Byrnes

59. Choice A: if only the second and third sets are exactly alike
3717 West **13**th Ave. 3717 West 18th Ave. 3717 West 18th Ave.

60. Choice B: if only the first and second sets are exactly alike
Donner Hill Road   Donner Hill Road   D**oan**er Hill Road

Completed Summary Tables

Table 4: Daily Analysis of Cases: Monday, Tuesday and Wednesday				
Status of Case	Monday	Tuesday	Wednesday	Total Cases
Adjourned	|||| 4	|||| 4	||||| 5	13
Defaulted	| 1	||| 3	|| 2	6
Dismissed	||| 3	||| 3	|| 2	8
Settled - with Money Award	||| 3	||| 3	||| 3	9
Settled- with NO Money Award	|| 2	||| 3	|||| 4	9
Total Cases	13	16	16	45
Cases by Year Filed				
2017	||| 3	||| 3	||| 3	9
2018	|||| 4	|||| || 7	||||| 5	16
2019	||||| | 6	||||| | 6	||||| ||| 8	20
Total Cases	13	16	16	45

Table 5: Summary of Cases from Monday - Wednesday						
Part	Case Status at End of Day					Total Cases
	Adjourned	Defaulted	Dismissed	Settled With Money Award	Settled No Money Award	
A	||||| ||| 8	| 1		|||| 4	| 1	14
B	| 1	|| 2	|| 2	|| 2	||||| 5	12
C	||| 3	| 1		|| 2	|| 2	8
D	| 1	|| 2	||||| | 6	| 1	| 1	11
Total	13	6	8	9	9	45

61. A. Adjourned (13)

62. B. 2 (8 - 6 = 2)

63. C. 29 (9 + 20 = 29)

64. D. 2019 (20)

65. C. 45 (13 + 16 + 16 = 45)

66. D. none of the above (8)

67. C. Part D (6)

68. B. Part C

69. D. none of the above (Adjourned 13 + "Defaulted" 6 = 19)

70. A. Part A (14 cases)

71. C. Part C (2 and 2)

72. B. 2017 (9)

73. D. none of the above (3)

74. D. none of the above ("Adjourned" 13 + "Defaulted" 6 + "Dismissed" 8 = 27)

75. C. Adjourned (13)

END OF ANSWERS FOR PRACTICE TEST 5

Made in the USA
Middletown, DE
02 September 2021

47388513R10075